SHE BELIEVES, SHE RECEIVES

SHE BELIEVES, SHE RECEIVES

A Powerful Guide to Courage, Clarity, and Abundance

JANINE CASCIO

RIVER GROVE
BOOKS

Published by River Grove Books
Austin, TX
www.rivergrovebooks.com

Distributed by River Grove Books

Design and composition by Greenleaf Book Group
Cover design by Greenleaf Book Group
Cover images © Adobe Stock / lankogal; © Adobe Stock / Yelyzaveta

Publisher's Cataloging-in-Publication data is available.

Print ISBN: 979-8-90052-019-3

eBook ISBN: 979-8-90052-020-9

First Edition

*To my family, who have been my constant
support and greatest blessing.*

*To my fiancé, whose love and encouragement
give me strength every day.*

*To my spiritual mentors, who have shared
wisdom that continues to guide me.*

*To my yoga practice, which opened the door to
presence, peace, and growth.*

*And to everyone who has touched my journey
and lifted my consciousness higher.*

*Most of all, this is dedicated to the belief I found
within myself—the quiet knowing that when we trust,
act, and keep faith, life responds with abundance.*

CONTENTS

PART 4 • She Receives: Gratitude, Flow, and Overflow

INTRODUCTION

I didn't plan to write this book. I felt called to write it.

I'm the youngest of four. Growing up in a big, loud, loving family taught me how to speak up—but it also taught me how easy it is to lose your voice trying to please everyone else. For a long time, I was the one who tried to be what everyone expected. The achiever. The fixer. The one who smiled even when something inside felt misaligned.

But somewhere between building a business and rebuilding myself, I discovered the one thing that changed everything: Authenticity is power. And once I found that, I couldn't keep it to myself.

This book was born out of a moment I'll never forget—one of those heart whispers you feel before you even understand it. I was on the phone with my sister, and through her tears, she said, *"I just want to believe in myself the way you do."* That hit me straight in the soul. It wasn't about money. It wasn't about titles. It was about belief—*self-belief.*

That's when I knew: I needed to write this book. Not as some polished CEO with all the answers but as a woman who's done the real work: the looking inward, the unlearning, the letting go of victimhood, the breaking free from limiting beliefs that whispered, "Who do you think you are?"

This is the book I wish I had had when I felt stuck on autopilot, living a life that looked good on paper but felt anything but aligned. It's the book I wrote so you don't have to keep second-guessing yourself, playing small, or waiting for permission to become the version of you that's already inside: bold, clear, unstoppable.

I'm Janine Cascio, CEO of Simplending Financial, a private lending firm I scaled from a vision into a multimillion-dollar company. We are a leader in the private lending sector, empowering our investors for growth and success. I'm also a mentor, speaker, and mindset coach who's worked with women from all walks of life—women ready to stop shrinking and start owning their space.

But more importantly, I'm a woman who chose growth over comfort, truth over perfection, and power over fear. I've launched ventures that soared and others that stretched me through failure. And through it all, I've seen one consistent truth: When a woman shifts her inner world, her outer world changes, too.

This book is my offering to you—and to every woman, like my sister, who knows she was made for more but isn't sure how to get there. Whether you're launching your first business or reshaping one that no longer fits, this book will help you clear the clutter, quiet the noise, and reconnect with the power that's already inside you.

WHAT TO EXPECT

This book is divided into four transformative parts:

Part 1: She Thinks—You'll learn how to shift your mindset, clarify your beliefs, and cultivate the mental resilience needed to dream bigger and believe deeper. This section delves into understanding your core intentions, shaping your identity, confronting fears and embracing courage, identifying inner blocks, and building daily habits that elevate your mindset. Each chapter in this part offers strategies to move from confusion to clarity.

Part 2: She Believes—We'll explore how self-belief is built, what it means to lead from within, and how to break through the invisible walls of doubt and fear. You will discover how to gather evidence of your capabilities, nurture relationships with "belief builders" who champion your vision, and transform limiting beliefs into powerful affirmations.

Part 3: She Acts—This is where belief becomes motion. You'll learn how to take aligned, consistent action with clarity, confidence, and purpose. This part guides you through overcoming both internal and external obstacles, maintaining consistency even when motivation wanes, and developing a strategic visibility plan to put your brand in front of the right people.

Part 4: She Receives—In this final section, you'll learn how to open yourself up to success, embrace abundance, and celebrate everything you've become. This part explores the power of gratitude, the art of living in flow, and the profound impact of giving back to others.

Each chapter offers mindset shifts, practical strategies, real-life stories, and science-backed insights to help you move from confusion to clarity, fear to action, and dreaming to receiving.

HOW TO USE THIS BOOK

This isn't just a book to read—it's an experience to live. As you read, you'll notice that each chapter ends with review questions. Of course, you don't have to answer them, but I promise your experience and transformation will happen much faster if you do. So I recommend having a notebook or journal nearby as you read to write down your answers to these review questions. That way, you can truly engage with the material and go back later to see how much you've grown.

Read at your own pace. Highlight the parts that hit your heart. Pause to reflect when a story stirs something in you. This book is here to be your mirror, your mentor, and your momentum.

By the end of this journey, you will believe differently, act with purpose, and receive what's been waiting for you all along.

Let's get started.

A WOMAN'S POWER, PASSION, AND PURPOSE

CHAPTER 1

HARNESSING YOUR PASSION

Don't ask yourself what the world needs. Ask yourself
what makes you come alive, and go do that. Because what
the world needs is people who have come alive.
—HOWARD THURMAN

There are moments in life when we feel pulled toward something bigger than ourselves. It might be a dream we've carried for years, a spark of inspiration that won't fade, or a vision that feels impossible to ignore. That inner pull is more than passion—it's the beginning of transformation.

WHAT SETS YOUR SOUL ON FIRE?

Imagine that you own your own business, doing something you love. You've dreamed of starting this business for years, because you didn't want to just go through the motions. You wanted to create meaningful work that matters to you every day. You're working in your dream industry—maybe even one where women are often overlooked—yet here you are, breaking down barriers, leading with confidence, and feeling inspired in all that you do. Can you see it? I can. That's passion.

Without it, you'll end up chasing after goals that don't excite you. You'll spend countless nights working, facing disappointment, and wondering if what you're doing is actually worth all your effort. I don't want you to burn out like this. I know, because I've been there. Once I found my deep passion, everything changed, and I began building the business and life of my dreams.

Passion is a deep pull you feel toward something or someone you love, value, and are willing to pour your time and energy into.

One of the biggest misconceptions you might have about passion is thinking you need to find it—as if it's hiding somewhere, just waiting for you to stumble across it. But passion isn't a buried treasure. It is something you spark. It's already inside you; you just need to uncover it, nurture it, and direct it. That's where leadership begins—by aligning your inner fire with purposeful action and showing others what's possible.

In this chapter, you'll learn what true passion really means, how to uncover what sets your soul on fire, and how to nurture it until it fuels everything you do. You'll discover why igniting your passion is the first step to creating a life and business you truly love—and how this inner fire can guide your actions, inspire your leadership, and light the way for others to follow.

Look at What Energizes You

Think about the topics that friends and family often seek your advice on. Do your friends and colleagues often seek your advice on business matters, look to you for creative ideas, or ask for help with solving problems? It's pretty common for our natural talents and interests to line up with what we're really passionate about. If you enjoy helping others in a particular way, it's likely that your passion is tied to that experience. And often, that passion is the foundation of leadership—showing up where others look to you for guidance.

Another clue is in the topics you can talk about for hours and still find interesting. What topics really get you excited to speak on? What types of books, articles, or podcasts do you find yourself drawn to? You'll often recognize your passion through your own curiosity and enthusiasm. If something excites you enough to keep learning and growing, it might be the key to unlocking what truly sets your soul on fire. When you lead with curiosity, others are naturally drawn to follow.

Your daily life is full of hints about what you're passionate about. It shows up in those times when you feel totally alive, really engaged, and super excited. Have you ever found yourself so caught up in something that you completely lose track of time? You know, those moments when you glance at the clock and realize hours have flown by without you even realizing it? That's what passion looks like in action! These are often the same moments when your leadership begins to take shape—without you even realizing it.

For me, I figured out pretty early that I enjoyed helping people push through their limits. I've always been passionate about helping people transform and reach their full potential, whether it was through my work in finance, my time as a yoga and meditation teacher, or just mentoring those around me. That passion turned into the driving force behind my career. And over time, that passion became leadership—rooted in service, growth, and the desire to see others rise.

WHY YOU NEED TO FIND YOUR PASSION FOR YOUR BUSINESS

Passion is often what separates entrepreneurs who persevere through setbacks from those who walk away. It's a driving force that fuels persistence when sales are slow, when investors say no, or when your first launch flops. Passion is what gets you out of bed at five a.m. to tweak your marketing strategy or learn a new skill after everyone else has clocked out. And when others see that level of dedication, it inspires them, and it positions you as a leader in your business or community.

STRONG, AUTHENTIC PARTNERSHIPS

Passionate people attract more passionate people. Collaboration with individuals and brands who share your enthusiasm and beliefs is one of the most effective methods to build your business. But here's the thing: Don't just network for the sake of it. Create partnerships that are truly aligned with your mission.

Let's assume you run a handcrafted jewelry business. Instead of focusing solely on selling your items, consider how you may partner with other motivated businesses that share your goal. Consider collaborating with a sustainable fashion brand to establish an exclusive jewelry line that promotes ethical fashion. Or you could collaborate with a bridal boutique to provide customized wedding accessories or with local artists to create unique statement pieces.

These relationships bring in more clients and also allow you to broaden your reach in an authentic way. People will naturally gravitate toward your company if they see your enthusiasm and the heart behind it.

So instead of simply asking, *Who can help me grow?* consider, *Who shares my passion, and how can we grow together?*

Start by putting yourself in the right environments—places where passionate, driven entrepreneurs naturally show up. This might be a local event, a business workshop, or a women-led networking group. It could even be an online space, like a Facebook group or a forum where people talk about the kind of work that excites you. Listen closely to how people speak about their journey. When someone's eyes light up over the same things that matter to you, that's your cue. Reach out. Be curious. Have real conversations. The most meaningful partnerships often begin with a shared sense of purpose and a simple, genuine connection.

THE SCIENCE BEHIND PASSION

Neurobiologically, passion activates the brain's reward system, particularly areas associated with pleasure and the neurotransmitter dopamine. When you engage in passionate activities like painting, writing, building a business, or mentoring others, you activate these brain regions, bringing feelings of joy and satisfaction.[1]

Furthermore, passion is not merely a spontaneous emotion; it involves a complex interplay of brain circuits, genetics, neurotransmitters, and hormones. For instance, research suggests that genetic factors can influence personality traits like novelty seeking and persistence, which shape how intensely a person may pursue certain passions.[2] Hormones such as dopamine and oxytocin also play a key role—dopamine fuels motivation and reward-seeking behavior, while oxytocin, often called the "bonding hormone," strengthens emotional connections to people or work we deeply care about. When you understand these mechanisms, you're empowered to make informed choices, actively pursue your interests, and lead a more fulfilling life.

From a psychological perspective, the Dualistic Model of Passion, introduced by Robert J. Vallerand, delineates two types of passion: harmonious and obsessive.[3] This model shows how the nature of your passion can deeply influence your psychological health and behavior. Harmonious passion arises when you engage in activities you love freely, which leads to positive outcomes like well-being and personal growth. This kind of passion doesn't define who you are—it can enrich your life and help you become your most authentic self.

In contrast, obsessive passion occurs when your activity overpowers your identity—you start letting your passion define who you are and where you belong in the world. You may feel high self-esteem when you're engaged in your passion, but you can also experience guilt, shame, and burnout.[4] This type of burnout often stems from the pressure to constantly perform or succeed, leaving little room for rest or detachment. For example, a business owner might feel driven to work long hours every day—not out of joy, but from an internal fear of falling behind or being seen as inadequate. According to *Psychology Today*, obsessive passion can lead to a rigid persistence, even when the activity starts to interfere with health, relationships, or emotional well-being.[5] On the other hand, someone with harmonious passion might still work hard, but they know when to pause, recharge, and return with renewed energy—making their passion a source of growth rather than exhaustion.

Your passion comes from a dynamic interaction between how your mind works and how your brain functions. Recognizing the dualistic nature of passion and understanding that not all passion is beneficial can help you reflect on your own motivations. Are you pursuing your goals from a place of joy and alignment, or are you driven by pressure, fear, or identity attachment? Knowing the difference empowers you to channel your passion in ways that enhance your well-being rather than deplete it. This awareness is especially important for entrepreneurs, athletes, and high achievers, who may unintentionally let their work or calling consume their sense of self. By staying mindful of these patterns, you can build a life that is not only driven but also balanced and fulfilling.

THE PASSION MAP

Without direction, passion can feel disorganized or overwhelming. That's where your Passion Map comes in. A Passion Map is like a business plan for turning your ideas into successful businesses; it's a road map for your future. It helps you channel your passion into something important. By drawing out what drives and interests you, you can gain clarity, set meaningful goals, and build a life that fits your true calling.

Step 1: List Your Passions

The first step to making a Passion Map is pretty straightforward but very important: Write down all the things that get you excited and energized. Don't just stick to career-related interests—add your hobbies, the causes that matter to you, the skills that really make you come alive, and even the activities you enjoyed as a child. This step is similar to identifying your "Zone of Genius," a concept introduced by Gay Hendricks in *The Big Leap*, which refers to the unique combination of talents and passions that allow you to operate at your highest level of contribution and joy.[6]

Following are some guiding questions to help you brainstorm:

- What activities make you lose track of time?
- What do people often seek your advice or help with?
- When do you feel the most fulfilled and happy?
- What kind of problems do you feel compelled to solve?

At this stage, don't worry about how your passions connect or whether they seem practical. The goal is simply to get them all down on paper. Once you have a list, you can start identifying patterns and deeper themes.

Step 2: Identify Common Themes

After making a list of your passions, step back and look for themes that keep recurring. Our deepest passions are often linked in ways we don't see at first. If you love sharing stories, making a difference in the world, and helping other people succeed, for example, you might find that your true calling is in motivational speaking, content writing, or coaching.

To find these connections, ask yourself these questions:

- Do any of my passions share a common purpose or outcome?

- Which ones naturally complement each other?

- How do these passions fit into different areas of my life—career, personal growth, community involvement?

Sometimes, you notice that themes pop up more from values than from particular activities. If a lot of your interests center on creativity, innovation, and self-expression, you might find yourself attracted to things like starting your own business, writing, or getting involved in the arts. Noticing these patterns can really guide you in making more thoughtful decisions about weaving your passions into your everyday life.

Step 3: Find Alignment Between Passion and Purpose

Although passion is strong on its own, it becomes unstoppable when paired with your "why"—your deeper purpose. The key question you should answer with the use of your Passion Map is, *How can I incorporate these passions into my career or daily life?*

To achieve this, ask yourself these questions:

- What type of work allows me to utilize my passions on a daily basis?
- How can I incorporate more of my passions into my work, business, or personal life as it stands now?
- What are the chances that my passion could benefit others?
- Are there any voids in my personal or professional life that I could fill with activities motivated by my passions?

Don't panic if your current path doesn't match your passions. A major change in profession isn't always necessary for alignment; it might also involve beginning a side project, coaching others, or making minor regular changes to put your happiness first.

Step 4: Set Passion-Driven Goals

Now that you've identified your core passions and found alignment with your purpose, you'll be better able to set specific, actionable goals to move forward. Passion without planning might result in burnout. In Chapter 6 we will find out more about the SMART goals framework, a practical, proven method for setting goals that are specific, measurable, achievable, relevant, and time-bound. When you apply that framework to your passions, you'll begin to shape a vision that is both inspiring and actionable.

But we still have some work to do on our mindset before we set those goals.

For now, reflect on what matters most to you, and begin imagining what your next steps might look like. Keep your goals rooted in your passions, and as you move through this book, you'll gain the tools to make them real.

UNSURE OF WHAT SETS YOUR SOUL ON FIRE? IT'S TIME TO EXPERIMENT

Not sure what you're passionate about yet? That's okay—discovery takes movement. The key is to try different things and see what sparks your energy.

Here are some simple ways to start exploring:

- **Revisit old hobbies** you used to love as a child or teen.
- **Say yes to new experiences**—even ones that feel outside your comfort zone.
- **Take a class**, attend a workshop, or try a side project.
- **Volunteer** for a cause that interests you.
- **Talk to passionate people**—their excitement can be contagious.

Passion doesn't always arrive fully formed. Sometimes, it reveals itself when you take a leap into the unknown.

ALIGN YOUR PASSION AND PROFITABILITY

Loving what you do is wonderful, but let's be honest: You also need to make money. So, how can you transform your passion into a business that can sustain you?

Start with market research. Before venturing into any business, explore your industry. Use tools like Google Trends, Reddit, or Quora to find out what questions your potential customers are asking. Search keywords related to your passion and look at existing products or services. If your passion lies in finance or investing, examine niches like budgeting for families, crypto education, or retirement planning. Look at what's trending, what's lacking, and where there's growing interest.

Identify what your customers are willing to invest in. Your business is only as successful as people's willingness to pay for your offer. If you love making handmade candles, research what types sell best. If you're in the coaching industry, find out which products or services solve real problems for customers.

Test your idea. Ideas are great, but you'll need to see whether they'll work in practice. Test your concept on a small scale before diving in. Are you passionate about coaching? Provide a free session to see how people will respond. Do you enjoy designing clothing? Sell a limited batch before launching the entire collection.

IGNITE IT. DON'T WAIT FOR IT.

Passion is not something you stumble upon—it's something you ignite, nurture, and channel into purpose. It's the fuel that keeps you moving forward when challenges arise and motivation fades. True passion is about finding what energizes you, aligning it with a meaningful purpose, and allowing it to drive you through obstacles with resilience and determination.

Remember, it evolves over time. Stay open to growth, try new things, and be willing to adapt as you learn more about yourself. When passion aligns with purpose, setbacks become stepping stones and success becomes inevitable.

So, as you move forward, don't wait for passion to find you. Take action, embrace the process, and allow your passion to become the unstoppable force that propels you toward a life filled with meaning, excitement, and achievement.

REVIEW QUESTIONS

1. What does it mean to "pay attention to your sparks," and how can this help in discovering your passion?

2. What is the difference between finding passion and sparking passion, according to the chapter?

3. What role does curiosity play in discovering and sustaining passion?

4. How can journaling and reflecting on what energizes you aid in uncovering your true passion?

5. Why is it important to connect passion with purpose, and how can this drive success?

6. How can passion help push through fear and fuel resilience in the face of adversity?

7. How do fear and doubt hinder the pursuit of passion, and what strategies can help overcome them?

8. Why is it important to embrace the idea that your passion may evolve over time?

9. What are some ways to reignite your passion during challenging times?

PURSUING YOUR PURPOSE

A life without purpose is like a ship without a rudder.
—THOMAS CARLYLE

We all have things we love—the sparks that light us up and make us feel alive. But passion by itself can sometimes feel scattered—exciting in the moment, but without a clear direction. Purpose is what grounds that fire. It's the "why" behind the "what," the reason your passion keeps calling you back. When you start to bring those two together—what excites you and what gives your life meaning—you create a path that feels both fulfilling and unstoppable.

CONNECTING YOUR PASSION TO YOUR PURPOSE

Just having passion isn't quite enough; it needs direction. The most successful people don't just chase their passions aimlessly; they focus them into something meaningful. When your passion is linked, your purpose becomes very powerful—it's not just about you but about making a difference in the lives of others, too. This is often where influence begins. When passion meets purpose, others begin to rally around your vision because they feel it.

When I built Simplending Financial, my passion for breaking barriers and creating opportunities became my purpose. It was about empowering other women to believe in their abilities, overcome limiting beliefs, and build the confidence to take control of their financial future and business success. The more I aligned my business with this deeper mission, the more success naturally followed. I saw firsthand how passion connected to purpose could drive me through challenges, push me past doubt, and make every victory—big or small—feel incredibly rewarding. That kind of clarity fuels progress and inspires trust. People are more willing to follow someone whose purpose reaches beyond personal gain.

Ask yourself: *How can my passion create value? Who can benefit from what I love to do?* For example, if you're passionate about fitness, could you use that passion to help others achieve their health goals? If you love storytelling, could you channel that into writing, filmmaking, or coaching others on how to tell their stories? If you're fascinated by technology, could you create solutions that make people's lives easier or more efficient?

When your passion serves a bigger purpose, it becomes an unstoppable force in your life. It gives you a reason to push through the hard days and stay committed when things get tough. Purpose-driven passion keeps you going even when motivation fades.

And when others see that kind of consistency, they begin to admire it. In fact, they're moved by it. That's how movements start.

In this chapter, you'll discover how to move from simply having passion to living with a clear purpose. You'll learn how to connect what excites you to what truly matters, how to define the bigger impact you want to make, and why a purpose-driven life not only fuels your motivation but also inspires others to believe in your vision and join you on the journey.

DISCOVERING YOUR WHY

At its core, your purpose is really your "why" for starting and running your business. So let's dig into your deep "why."

If you ask most entrepreneurs why they started their business, you'll hear things like

- "I want to make a lot of money."

- "I want more freedom."

- "I want to be successful."

But those aren't really your "whys"—those are *outcomes*. They're results of something deeper, something more personal to you.

For example, let's say your first answer is "I want financial success." Ask yourself, *Why?* Maybe it's because you want to provide for your family in a way that your parents never could. Maybe it's because you grew up watching your mom struggle to make ends meet, and you vowed that your own children would never experience that. Or maybe you experienced financial hardship yourself, and now you're determined to never feel that powerless again.

That's a real "why." That's something that will keep you going when things get hard. And it's from that deeply personal place that many leaders draw their courage, vision, and grit.

Maybe your answer is "I want to be my own boss." Again, *why?* Is it because you hate being told what to do? Or is it deeper than that? Maybe you spent years in a toxic work environment where your talents were overlooked, and now you want to create a business where people, especially women, feel valued, seen, and heard. That drive to build something better for others sets the tone for the culture you create and the people you inspire.

If you stop at surface-level answers, you'll never fully connect with the fire inside you. But when you dig deep enough, you'll uncover a "why" that's so powerful, so personal, that quitting will never be an option.

THE POWER OF THE FIVE WHYS

One of the simplest yet most powerful ways to uncover your "why" is the "Five Whys" method, a problem-solving technique developed by Taiichi Ohno at Toyota shortly after World War II to identify the root causes of problems in manufacturing. It's now widely used to uncover personal motivations as well.

This exercise forces you to go beyond the surface level and find the emotional core behind your "why." Each "why" brings you closer to clarity and the beliefs that shape your decisions. And clarity is what enables strong, purpose-led leadership.

Whether you're leading a team or building a vision from the ground up, understanding your deepest motivations makes your direction easier to follow and your message harder to ignore. Here is how you can use it to uncover the purpose behind starting your business:

1. Start with what you want to do. Example: "I want to start my own business."

2. Ask yourself: *Why do I want to start this business?* Example: "Because I want to work for myself and have more freedom."

3. Ask why that freedom matters to you. Example: "Because I want to spend more quality time with my family and create a life on my own terms."

4. Ask why creating that kind of life is important. Example: "Because I grew up watching my parents struggle, and I want to break that cycle for my children."

5. Ask why breaking that cycle really matters to you. Example: "Because I want to build a legacy of hope and possibility—to show my family and others that we can rise above our circumstances."

When you ask "why" for the fifth time, you're probably going to find something really personal. Something emotional. That's your real "why."

THE SCIENCE OF PURPOSE

We often think of purpose as something abstract—an emotional or a spiritual concept. But science has increasingly confirmed that having a sense of purpose is also a powerful predictor of mental, physical, and emotional well-being.

Purpose Strengthens Physical and Mental Health

A growing body of research links purpose with better health and well-being. For example, a 2023 meta-analysis published in the *Journal of Clinical Psychology* reviewed studies on purpose in life and found that individuals with a strong sense of purpose consistently reported lower levels of depression and anxiety.[1] Other recent studies show that purpose is also connected to healthier behaviors—such as more frequent exercise, better nutrition, and lower rates of substance use—which may help explain why people with high purpose often experience greater overall health and functioning.[2]

Purpose May Protect the Brain from Cognitive Decline

According to an article in *Practical Neurology*, people with a higher sense of purpose are less likely to develop Alzheimer's disease or other forms of dementia.[3] Neurologists are increasingly recognizing that purpose contributes to what's called "cognitive reserve"—the brain's ability to maintain function even when faced with aging or neurological damage.

One study referenced in the article found that older adults with strong purpose scores had a 30 percent reduced risk of cognitive impairment compared to their peers.

YOUR STRUGGLES SHAPE YOUR PURPOSE

Every successful entrepreneur, leader, or changemaker has a story of struggle. Oprah was fired from her first TV job and told she wasn't fit for television. Sara Blakely, the founder of Spanx, spent years facing rejection before her product finally gained traction. Howard Schultz, the man who turned Starbucks into a global brand, grew up in public housing and experienced the kind of financial hardship that later fueled his vision. In the early 1990s, as he led Starbucks through its early expansion, Schultz leaned into creating a company that offered health-care benefits and stock options even to part-time employees—a bold move at the time that reflected a people-first philosophy.

Their struggles didn't break them; instead, those struggles redefined them. They shaped their purpose, their vision, and their relentless drive to succeed.

Let's face it, nobody likes struggling. It is difficult to find the lesson in a difficult season when you are in the middle of one. You are merely trying to survive, to keep on, to cross to the other side. But perspective is a gift from the past. And when you lead others, that perspective becomes a light you carry for those walking through their own shadows.

Consider a moment in your life when you had to face something challenging. Perhaps it was rejection, financial difficulty, the death of a loved one, failure, or a significant personal setback. At the time, it felt unjust. It felt like something you had to endure. But looking back, can you see what it taught you?

Perhaps it imparted to you resilience, patience, or ingenuity. Perhaps it changed your viewpoint on what truly counts or let you see a greater degree of empathy.

If you struggled financially growing up, for instance, that experience might have motivated you to build a better future for others as well as for yourself. If you were repeatedly turned down, perhaps that experience helped you learn perseverance and today gives you the confidence to pursue your most ambitious goals.

Struggles don't just happen to you; they happen for you. They shape you into who you're meant to become. And they often point directly to your "why."

If you're trying to discover your personal "why," start with your hardest moments. Think about the challenges that tested you the most, the moments when you felt like giving up, the experiences that shaped how you see the world.

Because more often than not, your "why" is hidden inside those struggles.

THE CONNECTION BETWEEN YOUR DEEP WHY AND YOUR PERSONAL VALUES

Your deep "why" doesn't stand alone—it's rooted in your values.

Think of your "why" as the fuel and your *values* as the compass. Purpose gives you energy, but values give you direction. When your purpose aligns with what you truly value, it becomes a mission that you live and lead by.

For example, if your "why" is about helping others achieve financial freedom, your core values might include *empowerment*, *independence*, and *integrity.* These values then influence how you run your business, how you treat your clients, and even the types of products or services you offer.

Let's break this down even more.

If you value honesty, you'll naturally prioritize transparent communication with clients or customers, even when it's uncomfortable or costs you in the short term.

If you value creativity, you'll build a brand that stands out with fresh thinking, innovation, and authentic storytelling.

If you value justice or equality, your business might focus on underrepresented communities, fair pricing, or inclusive hiring practices.

When your purpose and values are in sync, you're no longer guessing what kind of business to build; you're designing a business that reflects who you are at your core.

This clarity also strengthens your leadership. People are drawn to leaders who are consistent or those who walk their talk. Your values become your brand's backbone, and your deep "why" becomes the driving force that inspires others to trust and follow your vision.

Take time to name your values clearly. What principles do you want your life and business to embody? Write them down. Then ask yourself: *How does my purpose reflect these values? How can my business become an extension of what I believe in? How can I lead in a way that reinforces these values in everyday decisions?*

When your deep "why" is filtered through the lens of your values, you'll lead with more authenticity, clarity, and conviction. And you'll not only build a business but a legacy.

IMPACT AND LEGACY

When your purpose aligns with your values, it naturally shapes the impact you have on others—and that impact becomes your legacy. When you know what change you want to make, you stop thinking about what you can do for yourself and start thinking about what you can do for others. Nothing can stop you once you know the impact you want to make and the effect you want your business and work to have on the people you serve.

So ask yourself: *What do I want people to remember about me? What kind of change do I want to make? How can I help other people through my journey?*

After all is said and done, success is short-lived, but impact lasts. When you define your impact, you define your purpose. And once you have a clear purpose, nothing can stand in your way.

APPLYING YOUR PURPOSE TO YOUR BUSINESS'S MISSION

Once you've uncovered your deep "why" and clarified your values, the next step is to apply them directly to your business mission. Your mission is a declaration of leadership. It's how you translate your purpose into action and direction.

Your business mission should answer these questions:

- What are you here to do?

- Who are you here to serve?

- How will you serve them in a way that reflects your purpose and values?

Let's say your deep "why" is "I want to help busy parents create a better work-life balance, so they can spend more time with their children." Your core values might be *family, freedom, simplicity,* and *honesty.* A mission that applies this purpose might be: *to empower working parents with flexible solutions that simplify their lives, support their well-being, and give them more time for what matters most—family.*

Notice how that mission isn't vague. It's grounded in purpose, directed by values, and speaks to a specific audience. It gives clarity to you, your team, and your customers about what you're building and why.

Mission Drives Leadership

A clear mission is what transforms you from a dreamer into a leader. Without a mission, you're reactive. With a mission, you're intentional.

When you articulate your mission and live it out in your brand, your messaging, and your service delivery, people will start to look to you as someone who is leading with conviction. And that's where leadership starts—not in a title or position but in purpose-driven action.

You don't have to be the loudest in the room, but you do have to be the clearest on your "why" and the most committed to living it out. That's what builds trust. That's what inspires people to follow your vision, buy into your brand, and stay loyal to your business.

Take the following actions to craft your business mission:

1. Write your deep "why" in one sentence.
   Example: I believe no child should grow up without access to quality education.

2. List your top three to five personal values.
   Example: equality, innovation, service, impact

3. Write your mission statement by combining the two.
   Example: To create accessible educational tools that inspire underprivileged children to learn, grow, and thrive.

Don't overthink the wording. What matters most is clarity and authenticity. As your business grows, your mission may evolve, but the core should remain consistent with your purpose and values.

When your business mission is built on your deep "why," you automatically lead from a place of meaning. You make stronger decisions. You build stronger connections. And you become the kind of leader who creates a lasting impact.

PASSION + PURPOSE = LIMITLESS SUCCESS

When your passion and purpose align, you gain clarity. Your Passion Map becomes a guide for making choices that match your values and goals. Ask yourself: *What energizes me? How can I use that to create value for others?* That clarity drives consistent, meaningful progress.

EMBRACING YOUR WHY AND MOVING FORWARD

You don't have to come up with a perfect answer to find your "why"; you just have to dig deep and be honest with yourself. Finding out what really drives you, what really excites you, and what gives your work value beyond just making money or getting approval from other people is important. Everything changes when you align your actions with that bigger goal. You're not just going through the motions anymore. Instead, you move with clarity, confidence, and conviction.

Consider the difference between working just to make ends meet and working toward something that really motivates you. You don't just work hard when you know your "why"; you work with purpose. You no longer question your decisions, compare yourself to other people's journeys, or wonder if you're on the right track. You know you are because your actions are in line with what you really care about. Everything starts to fall into place once you find it and fully accept it. Problems are turned into learning opportunities, and each victory is more satisfying when you know it's not just about you.

So, what's your "why"? What fuels you and keeps you going when things get tough?

REVIEW QUESTIONS

1. What is the difference between surface-level goals and a deeper personal "why"?

2. According to the chapter, why should your "why" evoke strong emotions?

3. Why is it important to reflect on moments when you felt most alive or fulfilled?

4. What role do personal struggles and challenges play in uncovering your deeper purpose?

5. How can identifying problems that trouble you so deeply help you find your purpose?

6. Why is it important for your "why" to be bigger than just personal gain?

7. What is the connection between your deep "why" and your personal values, and how does this shape your vision and business goals?

8. How can applying your purpose to your business mission give you direction and clarity?

9. In what ways does having a strong sense of purpose help you step into the leadership role required to run a successful business?

10. How does having a clear "why" help entrepreneurs stay motivated during tough times?

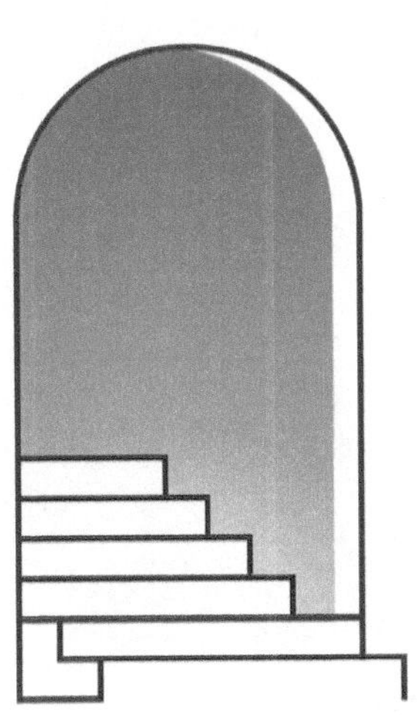

SHE THINKS:
HARNESSING MINDSET TO VISUALIZE YOUR SUCCESS

DEVELOPING THE RIGHT MINDSET

The mind is everything. What you think you become.
—BUDDHA

When I launched my first business, I was delighted, but afraid. Every step seemed like walking a tightrope, and self-doubt crept in every day. *What if I fail? What if I am not cut out for this?* These thoughts clouded my mind. Then, one day, I spoke with a mentor who said, "Your mindset will either be the wind in your sails or the anchor that drags you down." That struck a chord because it made me realize that my biggest obstacle wasn't my lack of experience or resources; it was my own thoughts holding me back. It was a wake-up call that if I wanted my business to move forward, I first needed to get out of my own way.

From that point forward, I decided to shift my focus from fear to possibility. I stopped worrying about failing to attract customers, running out of funds, or making a costly mistake that would ruin everything.

Instead, I began focusing on what could go well, such as the excitement of building something new, the potential to help others, receiving positive feedback from a customer, or successfully launching a new product. I learned to appreciate the little things that went well and to view failures as lessons rather than losses. It didn't happen all at once, but over time, work began to feel more enjoyable, and success appeared more likely.

The point is, everyone wants to succeed, whether you are a business owner, an athlete, or a student. But a strong mind is at the heart of every success story. It's what sets the extraordinary apart from the ordinary. How far you can go and the direction your life takes depend on how you think. If I hadn't accepted this, I might still be stuck in doubt, missing out on opportunities.

So, how can you tell if you're stuck in a limiting mindset? It often shows up through negative self-talk, like constantly doubting your abilities or expecting failure before you even begin. You might procrastinate, avoid taking risks, or fear stepping out of your comfort zone. People with a stuck mindset often focus on past mistakes, comparing themselves to others and feeling inadequate. Recognizing these patterns is your first step toward breaking free—because awareness allows you to challenge these thoughts and replace them with a mindset geared toward growth and possibility.

In this chapter, you'll learn how to cultivate the right mindset for success. You'll learn about the difference between a fixed and growth mindset and why adopting a growth mindset is crucial for overcoming challenges and achieving your goals.

WHAT IS MINDSET?

Have you ever wondered why some people do well when faced with challenges, while others step back or fumble? It could be because of their mindset.

Your *mindset* refers to the way you view and think about the traits that make up your personality. It's also a set of beliefs that shape how you make sense of the world and yourself. It influences how you think, feel, and behave in any given situation. It means that what you believe about yourself impacts your success or failure. Your mindset affects how you learn, handle setbacks, and reach success.

Your mindset can influence how you behave in a wide range of life situations. For example, as you encounter different situations, your mind triggers a specific mindset that directly impacts your behavior.

The right mindset can be your greatest asset on your path to success, but a limiting one can be your greatest obstacle. When you have the right perspective, you'll enjoy your work and business, and success can become more attainable. Success isn't a limited resource—there's a lot to go around, and mastering your mindset is the key to unlocking it.

Is your mindset holding you back or propelling you forward? If you want to achieve success, you need to make a few adjustments to the way you think. Let's discover how.

TYPES OF MINDSETS

There are basically two types of mindsets: fixed and growth.

If you have a fixed mindset, you believe your inner abilities are permanent traits and therefore cannot be developed or changed. This suggests that your inner qualities, like intelligence and charisma, are set from birth. You might also believe that your talent and intelligence alone lead to success and that you don't need to put in extra effort to get where you want to be. You might also feel stuck and struggle to motivate yourself to make lasting changes.

In contrast, if you have a growth mindset, you believe your talents and inner abilities can be developed or changed over time. With this mindset, you don't necessarily believe you'll become Albert Einstein or Steve Jobs, but you do believe you can grow more intelligent or talented if you put in the effort. In other words, a growth mindset means you believe that these inner qualities can be improved through deliberate practice and learning.

For instance, as an aspiring entrepreneur, you'll need fundamental finance skills to develop your business's budget and prepare its financial statements. But maybe you weren't very good in math class or never had training in managing finances of any kind. If you adopt a fixed mindset, you might think, *I've never excelled in math, much less in financial statements. I'm not cut out for running my own business.*

Conversely, if you approach the situation with a growth mindset, you might think, *I don't have a background in finance, but I can learn. I'll develop my skills through learning and practice until I feel competent.*

Let's look at the differences between growth and fixed mindsets:

GROWTH MINDSET	FIXED MINDSET
Believes abilities can develop	Believes abilities are innate
Embraces challenges	Avoids challenges
Persists in the face of setbacks	Gives up easily
Adapts strategies to improve	Sticks to what feels comfortable
Takes risks to learn	Avoids risks to prevent failure
Views failure as a chance to grow	Sees failure as a reflection of self-worth
Focuses on progress	Focuses on perfection
Explores new opportunities	Stays within familiar boundaries
Welcomes constructive feedback	Avoids feedback to protect ego
Believes intelligence is expandable	Believes intelligence is static

If the column on the right sounds more like you, I encourage you to remember this: Mindset is everything when it comes to making a lasting change. Recognizing that truth is the very first step toward success.

THE SCIENCE BEHIND BUILDING A GROWTH MINDSET

Research from Stanford University demonstrates the power of developing the right mindset. Psychologist Carol Dweck and colleagues found that what you believe about yourself matters. The research revealed that students with a growth mindset see hard times as learning opportunities. They don't think intelligence is fixed, and they believe they can grow and become more intelligent. This way of thinking helps them excel in school. It also makes them better at solving problems.[1]

The mindset effect isn't just for school. It is also applicable at work:

- Forty-seven percent of employees in growth mindset companies report having more trustworthy colleagues.

- Sixty-five percent are more likely to say their company supports risk-taking.

- Forty-nine percent are more likely to say their organization encourages innovation.[2]

This shows how changing how you think can change a whole company. Believing you can grow opens up new opportunities and achievements.

Dweck's work demonstrates that with the right education and practice, you can shift and grow your mindset. This lets you tackle challenges and see failures as stepping stones to success.

WHY MINDSET MATTERS TO YOUR BUSINESS

Ladies, as an experienced entrepreneur with two successful businesses, I know the hurdles we face—where access to funding, industry bias, and balancing business with personal responsibilities can be daunting. But I also know the immense power we hold when we shift our mindset to growth and resilience. While a growth mindset can benefit anyone, it's especially essential for entrepreneurs.

Let me share with you how the right mindset can impact your success and how you can harness its power to launch and grow your business.

Helps You Improve on Your Product

One of the primary attributes of a growth mindset is the capacity to accept and develop from feedback. A growth mindset enables entrepreneurs to turn constructive criticism into a stepping stone for success. Entrepreneurs can further develop their products or services by identifying areas for improvement, making necessary modifications, and staying open to feedback. Entrepreneurs with a growth mindset actively seek feedback from customers, mentors, and colleagues. They comprehend the importance of constructive criticism as a valuable instrument for the expansion of their business and personal development.

Take the example of Anastasia Soare, the founder of Anastasia Beverly Hills. When she first introduced the Golden Ratio Eyebrow Shaping Method in the 1990s, many in the beauty industry were skeptical. At the time, eyebrows weren't considered an essential part of makeup, and most salons didn't offer specialized brow-shaping services. Some critics dismissed her approach as unnecessary, believing that eyebrows didn't need precise shaping.

Instead of getting discouraged, Soare refined her techniques by studying facial proportions and symmetry, using the Golden Ratio to design the perfect brow shape for each client. She worked closely with customers, adjusting her methods based on their feedback, and built a reputation as the go-to expert for eyebrows. Over time, as more celebrities and clients embraced her method, her brand grew into a global empire. If she'd remained in a fixed mindset, she would have never made these changes, to the detriment of her sales and her company.[3]

Helps You Take Calculated Risks

In addition, the capacity to take calculated risks is also stimulated by a growth mindset. Entrepreneurs with this perspective perceive risks as opportunities for expansion and development. They recognize that entrepreneurship is inherently risky and that their potential for success may be restricted if they refrain from taking risks.

For example, Brianne West, the founder of Ethique, a zero-waste beauty brand, made the bold decision to rebrand her company and focus on sustainable beauty products such as shampoo and conditioner bars packaged in recyclable paper rather than plastic. Despite initial challenges and skepticism from some investors, West believed in the long-term growth potential of eco-friendly products. Her willingness to take this calculated risk paid off when Ethique expanded to more than twenty countries, including Australia, the United States, Taiwan, and Hong Kong, achieving a turnover of more than $10 million a year by 2019.[4]

In order to uncover dormant markets, uncover new possibilities, and achieve greater heights, entrepreneurs must embrace risks and venture outside of their comfort zones.

Helps You Transition into New Fields

When you have a growth mindset, you don't allow your past experiences or skills to define your future. This can be an asset if you have expertise and experience in another field and want to pursue entrepreneurship.

For instance, Indya Wright started Artiste House, a PR and production company. She used to work as a commercial banker and as a deputy clerk at the Washington, DC, Superior Court. She didn't allow her former job to limit her potential. Instead, she knew that she could learn how to talk to people in the business world by doing things herself and taking a course on entrepreneurship fundamentals online. Today, Artiste House is a thriving full-service creative agency, securing major clients and media features, including a *Forbes* spotlight for celebrity barber Eric "Kleankut" Dixon and PR campaigns for companies like Geojam, which was highlighted in AfroTech, a leading media platform for Black tech innovators and entrepreneurs. Wright says, "You need to find ways to equip yourself with the skills necessary to sustain your business."[5]

Helps You Become More Resilient

A growth mindset makes you more resilient. *Resilience* is the ability to bounce back from setbacks, adapt to challenges, and keep moving forward despite difficulties. This quality is crucial because as an entrepreneur, you're bound to face obstacles—whether they come in the form of financial struggles, unexpected changes, or tough decisions. Your business's survival depends on your ability to persevere and learn from these difficult situations. When things get tough, you keep going and find new ways to solve problems.

Being resilient enables you to view these challenges as temporary and surmountable, pushing you to continue striving toward your goals rather than giving up. Rather than seeing setbacks as failures, view them as opportunities to learn and grow. When you believe you can improve through effort, that belief is key to becoming more resilient. It makes you brave and ready to face challenges. Entrepreneurs with this perspective embrace adversity as a chance to adapt, refine their strategies, and ultimately become stronger, making resilience a natural outcome of their mindset.

Take, for example, Ricardo Semler, who took over his father's company, Semco, in 1980. Facing a severe economic downturn in Brazil during the early 1990s, many companies declared bankruptcy. Instead of succumbing to the crisis, Semler implemented innovative management practices, including wage cuts agreed upon by workers in exchange for increased profit shares and significant salary reductions for management. These measures led to a 65 percent reduction in inventories and a decrease in product defects to less than 1 percent. By embracing these changes, Semco not only survived the economic turmoil but also experienced substantial growth, with annual revenue reaching $212 million by 2003.[6]

Helps You Embrace Challenges

A growth mindset is crucial for success because it determines how we perceive and respond to challenges. Embracing challenges means facing difficulties head-on instead of avoiding them and seeing setbacks as opportunities to learn and improve. This mindset pushes you to adapt, think creatively, and persist when things get tough—qualities every entrepreneur needs to succeed.

Conversely, if you fall into a fixed mindset, it can hold you back by creating fear of failure and resistance to change, as I've seen with others who couldn't move forward due to their limiting beliefs. For example, when I first started my journey as an entrepreneur, I faced significant challenges, particularly with cash flow management. Many of my clients struggled to secure funding for their businesses, and I had to find creative solutions to connect them with the right financial resources. There were times when deals fell through due to unexpected lender restrictions or when clients hesitated to move forward out of fear of debt.

I could have let this set me back, but instead, I shifted my mindset. I saw these struggles as opportunities to refine my business strategy, improve my financial planning, diversify funding sources, and build stronger relationships with my clients. This approach helped me push through difficult times—navigating complex negotiations, overcoming client hesitations, and finding alternative funding options when traditional lenders declined applications—ultimately leading to greater success.

That success meant securing a higher number of funding approvals for clients, increasing my firm's revenue, expanding my network of reliable lenders, and establishing Simplending Financial as a go-to resource for business financing.

Helps You Stay Humble

Finally, a growth mindset reminds you that there is always more to learn. This keeps you humble throughout your career path by reminding you that there is always more room for improvement. Humility helps you avoid stagnation, fosters better teamwork, and makes it easier to accept constructive feedback. It also encourages you to listen to others' ideas, which can lead to innovation and stronger relationships with employees and customers.

Importantly, humility is not the same as downplaying your abilities or pretending you don't know anything. It means recognizing your strengths while staying open to new knowledge and being willing to admit mistakes and adjust.

Customers' demands, needs, attitudes, and motives vary with time, therefore it's important to always review your product-market fit. If you become overly comfortable with your early expertise, you may miss opportunities to develop alongside your target audience and satisfy their requirements as they arise.

Let's look at Howard Schultz again, the former CEO of Starbucks. When Starbucks first expanded, it focused on selling coffee beans and equipment rather than operating cafés. Instead of assuming this model was perfect, Schultz studied European coffee culture and saw an opportunity for his business in the United States. He humbled himself, learned from others, and transformed Starbucks into a global coffeehouse chain centered on customer experience.

Later, when Starbucks faced declining sales during the 2008 financial crisis, Schultz once again demonstrated humility. Rather than blaming external factors, he admitted the company had lost touch with its customers. He reinvested in barista training, improved product quality, and redesigned stores—all because he was willing to listen and adapt. This approach helped Starbucks recover and thrive.[7]

TOOLS FOR DEVELOPING A GROWTH MINDSET

Now that we've explored why developing a growth mindset is essential in building your business, let's look at how you can do it.

Think of your brain as a muscle. You must train your brain through intentional practice and attention, and you need to give it consistent care and effort to grow stronger. We do that through focusing on building the right identity rather than worrying about getting the right result.

This is how you develop a resilient, focused mental attitude (growth mindset). Here are twelve effective ways and tools to develop a growth mindset.

1. Be Willing

Remember, your thoughts are yours to control, and you have the power to change them. This is the essence of personal power: choice and responsibility. Embrace the willingness to change. Be bold in your decisions. Be open to making choices and ready to take on challenges with courage and determination.

As Viktor Frankl beautifully expressed in *Man's Search for Meaning*,

"Everything can be taken from a person but one thing: the last of the human freedoms—to choose one's attitude in any given set of circumstances, to choose one's own way."[8]

2. Feed the Mindset You Want

The quickest way to shift your mindset is to actively nurture the one you wish to develop. The next time you feel yourself resisting change or feeling negative about your efforts, take a pause. Are these thoughts helping you or hindering you? How could you shift to a more growth-oriented frame of mind instead?

Research shows that interventions reinforcing a growth mindset are associated with reductions in fixed-mindset beliefs.[9] Professional athletes and top performers have known this for years. They devote as much time to their mental state as their physical training, usually with their own mindset coaches and strategies to feed the right mindset for performing at their best. You don't need to hire a mindset coach to make real change; you just need to be aware of your thoughts and shift them to be more willing, open, and positive.

3. Listen to and Challenge Your Inner Voice

Start by truly listening to your inner voice. If you struggle to hear your inner voice, start by creating quiet moments in your day. Try a few minutes of journaling or meditation to clear your mind. Ask yourself questions like, *What am I really feeling?* or *Is this belief helping me grow?* Writing your thoughts down can reveal patterns and help you tune in. Once you hear your inner voice, challenge it. Replace limiting beliefs with growth mindset statements to shift your thinking in a positive direction.

Here's a list of questions to guide you in adopting a growth mindset:

- What can I learn from this?

- What steps can I take to help me succeed?

- What information can I gather? And from where?

- Where can I get constructive feedback?

- If I had a plan to be successful at [blank], what might it look like?

- When will I follow through on my plan?

- Where will I follow through on my plan?

- How will I follow through on my plan?

- What mistake did I make that taught me something?

- Is my current learning strategy working? If not, how can I change it?

- What habits must I develop to continue the gains I've achieved?

After you answer these questions, take a moment to reflect on your responses. Look for insights and patterns in what you've written, and think about how you can adjust your perspective or approach to keep developing a growth mindset. Use your answers as a road map to challenge old beliefs and build new, empowering habits.

4. Practice Meditation

If you ask successful and high-achieving people about their habits and routines, they'll often say that they practice meditation. Many people claim they "don't have time" to meditate, but what if meditation could actually give us more time? It clears the mind, improves focus, and boosts productivity. Research consistently shows that meditation improves productivity, simplifies decision-making, and reduces stress.[10] Making this your daily habit is important for developing a success mindset.[11]

If you're new to meditation, start small; even five minutes a day can help. You can find beginner-friendly guided meditations on free apps like Headspace or Insight Timer, or simply search for short sessions on YouTube. Choose what works best for you and commit to it daily to build a strong foundation for success.

5. Build a Support Network

As an entrepreneur or a leader, it can often feel as though you are fighting your battles alone, with no one truly understanding your unique challenges. It can be lonely at the top. One of the most effective ways to build your confidence is to recognize that you are not alone in your struggles and to actively seek feedback and support from others who face similar experiences. It's encouraging to know that others face similar difficulties and even more empowering to learn how they have overcome them and achieved success. How can you find mentors, business associates, peers, and team members who can assist you? Connecting with other women who share similar interests as yours can provide you with encouragement, ideas, and constructive feedback.

6. Have an Abundance Mentality

Many of us grow up with a scarcity mindset. From a young age, we were taught that life is a zero-sum game—there can only be one winner—that we need to compete, and that money doesn't grow on trees. It might even be that your family didn't have enough money or food when you were growing up, causing real scarcity in your life. These early experiences can shape how we view the world.

But a scarcity mindset can hold us back when building our business. We need to develop an abundance mindset, shifting from a mindset of lack to one that sees limitless possibilities. It's about understanding that success isn't finite; there is room for everyone to grow, collaborate, and succeed.

In order to cultivate this mindset, you must collaborate with others instead of competing with them. Seek win-win scenarios where everyone benefits. For example, you can partner with another small business to cross-promote each other's services, share resources, or cohost an event, so both of you reach new audiences and grow together. Embrace continuous learning and improvement, as this helps you stay adaptable and open to new ideas.

7. Don't Compare Yourself with Others

As much as we want to support other women, let's be honest—seeing others succeed can sometimes be triggering. When a colleague gets the promotion you were hoping for, or another business owner lands an amazing new client, it can leave you feeling less than.

On one hand, we genuinely want success for others. But on the other hand, it brings up feelings of unworthiness, self-doubt, and harsh self-criticism.

Instead, we need to focus on our own unique journey and remember that our individuality makes us incomparable. No one else has the same combination of gifts, challenges, strengths, privileges, and hardships that you do. Your path will look different from someone else's. You might be in a particular season of life, like the early stages of starting a business, or returning to work after maternity leave, feeling drained. Don't compare your winter to someone else's spring. Trust that your season will come, and focus on nurturing your own growth in the meantime.

8. Reprogram Your Subconscious Blocks with Positive Self-Talk

We all have thoughts that hold us back, even if we don't always realize it. These subconscious blocks—such as *I'm not good enough*, *I'll fail if I try*, or *I don't deserve success*—quietly limit what we think we can do. In business and leadership, they can stop us from moving forward, make us doubt ourselves, or even cause us to repeat the same mistakes.

In business and leadership, these beliefs can be especially damaging. They can lead to self-sabotage, repeating the same mistakes, or even holding yourself back from growth because of fear or doubt. Sometimes you're aware of these thoughts, but other times they're so ingrained you might not even realize they're there.

The good news? Once you recognize these thoughts, you can start to rewrite them. Whether it's through hypnotherapy, coaching, or other techniques, there are ways to shift these beliefs and clear the path forward. Reprogramming your mindset frees you to let go of what's been holding you back and opens the door to your next level of success.

9. Prioritize Learning over Approval

In life and work, it's easy to get caught up in seeking the approval of others. We often chase validation, hoping for a pat on the back or a reassuring nod that we're doing things "right." But shifting your focus from approval to learning can be transformative. Instead of worrying about what others think, ask yourself: *What can I learn from this experience?*

This shift in mindset reduces the fear of judgment that so often holds us back. When you prioritize learning, mistakes and setbacks no longer feel like failures. They become opportunities—stepping stones that lead to growth and improvement. By focusing on what each situation can teach you, you'll find yourself more willing to take on ambitious, creative challenges without the weight of needing others' approval.

10. Celebrate Effort, Not Just Results

It's natural to aim for success, but success isn't always immediate or linear. Instead of fixating solely on the outcome, make it a habit to recognize and honor the effort you put in. True mastery doesn't come overnight; it's the result of consistent effort over time.

Shifting your focus to the process helps you appreciate the journey, not just the destination. Whether it's a small step forward, a minor victory, or even a lesson learned from a setback, every bit of progress matters. Celebrate these moments—they're proof of your persistence and resilience.

By acknowledging and valuing effort, you build the motivation to keep going, even when the results aren't immediate. Over time, this mindset will help you develop not only the skills but also the confidence to tackle bigger goals and embrace the challenges that come with growth.

11. Embrace the Change

Embracing change isn't just about accepting it; it's about feeling truly excited and passionate about the new mindset you're working to create. The more passionate you are about the change, the easier it becomes to break old habits and build new ones. In fact, your body responds by releasing endorphins—the feel-good chemicals that help fuel your energy and enthusiasm. These endorphins do more than just make you feel good; they play a key role in how your brain learns and adapts to new information. It's like a natural boost that keeps you motivated and ready to tackle the challenges that come with transformation.

The next time you're feeling the push for change, tap into that excitement—your passion will give you the energy you need to make it happen!

THE POWER OF A GROWTH MINDSET

Developing a growth mindset is a powerful tool for both personal and professional growth. It allows you to embrace challenges, stay humble, and continually evolve. When you foster a mindset that sees opportunities in obstacles, welcomes feedback, and remains open to learning, you can overcome setbacks and keep advancing toward success.

Remember, growth is a continuous journey, and with persistence, resilience, and a positive attitude, you will see your efforts pay off. Whether it's in business, relationships, or personal goals, a growth mindset is essential to achieving long-term success.

REVIEW QUESTIONS

1. What is the primary difference between a growth mindset and a fixed mindset?

2. How can embracing challenges lead to growth and personal development?

3. Why is humility an important aspect of a growth mindset, and how can it contribute to success?

4. What role does meditation play in developing a success mindset?

5. How does the concept of an abundance mentality differ from a scarcity mindset?

6. What are some practical steps you can take today to start shifting toward a growth mindset in your life?

SETTING CLEAR INTENTIONS

Your intentions create your reality.

—WAYNE DYER

I n 2022, I had taken on a corporate funding initiative for small businesses—an opportunity that promised prestige, money, and growth. But soon, I was drowning in bureaucracy, stuck in endless meetings instead of making a real impact. One late night, exhausted and buried in reports, I had a wake-up call—I was busy but not moving toward my true mission. That experience showed me the power of setting clear intentions.

Until then, I had let my goals push me in many directions, saying yes to almost everything without asking, *Does this align with my vision?* Because of this lack of focus, I felt overwhelmed and made little meaningful progress, despite working hard. I often recall a Monday morning coaching session in early 2017 when my mentor, a seasoned financial strategist, asked me, "What are you really working toward?" It was a simple but deep question. I paused for a minute and realized I didn't have a clear answer for the first time in months.

That moment changed everything.

Maybe you've been there too. You've started a new business and found yourself completely overwhelmed and unfocused. You've said yes to every client and every opportunity in an attempt to make something stick, but now you're exhausted, and maybe you even want to give up entirely.

I'm here to ask you what my mentor did that day: What are you really working toward?

This is where setting clear intentions comes in. If you know where you stand and what you want, you can run your business and your life with confidence and conviction to get yourself to where you really want to be. Have you ever had one of those days where everything just seemed to flow effortlessly? You woke up feeling refreshed, handled challenges with ease, and ended the day feeling accomplished—even if you didn't check everything off your to-do list. That's the power of setting clear intentions.

In this chapter, you'll learn how setting clear intentions can transform your life and help you achieve your goals. It's about knowing what you want, why you want it, and how to channel your efforts to get them. When you set clear intentions for your business and entrepreneur life, you begin to consciously shape your life instead of life happening to you by chance.

THE DIFFERENCE BETWEEN INTENTIONS AND GOALS

Intentions and *goals* are often used interchangeably, but they are not the same. Goals are specific, measurable outcomes that you work toward within a set time frame. They provide structure and help you track progress. For example, setting a goal might sound like this: "I want to grow my business by 20 percent in the next year."

Intentions, on the other hand, are broader and more fluid. They reflect the guiding principles behind your actions and decisions rather than focusing solely on a destination. Intentions shape how you approach your journey rather than just defining where you want to end up. For instance, an intention might be: "I want to approach my work with passion and integrity." Unlike goals, intentions are not bound by deadlines or rigid structures; they provide a sense of purpose that guides your daily choices.

When I learned to set clear intentions alongside my goals, everything changed. Instead of chasing every opportunity, I started asking myself, *Does this align with my vision?* That simple shift allowed me to prioritize what truly mattered, leading to greater fulfillment and success.

THE SCIENCE BEHIND SETTING CLEAR INTENTIONS

Setting an intention isn't just some feel-good practice; it's deeply rooted in neuroscience. Unlike a rigid to-do list, intentions shape your mindset and guide your actions, helping you navigate the day with purpose and focus. When you set an intention, you create a mental framework that directs your energy and attention toward what truly matters. Recent neuroscience research supports this—when you set a clear intention, your brain shifts into a focused state, making it easier to notice opportunities, stay motivated, and move in the right direction.[1]

Your brain has a built-in filter called the reticular activating system (RAS)—a network that decides what information is important and what can be ignored.[2] It's a group of neurons (brain cells) responsible for our sleep-wake cycle, focus, and attention. Ever notice how when you're thinking about buying a new car, you suddenly see that model everywhere? That's your RAS in action.

When you set a clear intention—whether it's *I want to approach today with confidence* or *I will find creative solutions in my business*—your RAS tunes into everything that supports that mindset. You start noticing ideas, people, and opportunities that align with your focus.

Intentions also activate the prefrontal cortex, the part of your brain responsible for decision-making and self-control. This means that when you intentionally decide how you want to show up—whether as a patient leader, a resilient entrepreneur, or a more mindful parent—you're training your brain to make choices that align with that vision.

A study published in the journal *American Psychologist* found that people who set implementation intentions (deciding in advance how they want to act in a situation) were far more likely to follow through on their behaviors than those who simply relied on motivation.[3] In this way, your intentions really do shape your reality.

Setting intentions isn't just a mindset trick—it's a scientifically backed way to align your brain with the life you want to create. And the best part? There's no pressure to get it *perfect*. Unlike rigid plans, intentions give you flexibility while keeping you grounded in what truly matters.

So, before diving into your day, take a moment. What's the energy, mindset, or focus you want to bring into your life today? That simple act might just change everything.

ALIGNING INTENTIONS WITH YOUR VALUES

Intentions gain real power when they are grounded in your core values. Values are the deeply held beliefs that guide your decisions, shape your behavior, and define what fulfillment looks like for you. When your intentions are aligned with these values, your actions carry clarity and purpose.

Think back to the values you identified in Chapter 1. Perhaps they included integrity, creativity, growth, freedom, or compassion. Once you know your values, it gives your intentions direction; they are no longer vague desires but purposeful commitments.

For instance, if you value authenticity, your intention might be to communicate openly, even when it's uncomfortable. If you value balance, you might commit to protecting your time and energy more intentionally. These types of intentions help you stay focused and keep you aligned with who you truly are.

Before setting your next intention, pause and ask: Which value is this rooted in? When you lead with values, your intentions naturally support a more fulfilling and consistent life—both personally and professionally.

SETTING SHORT-TERM AND LONG-TERM INTENTIONS

Over the years, I've developed a system of setting various types of intentions that serve distinct purposes in both my personal and professional life. Depending on what I'm focusing on, these intentions help provide clarity and direction—whether for daily actions, specific projects, or long-term aspirations.

These three types of intentions will help you in your journey as a successful entrepreneur.

1. Daily Intentions

Daily intentions are small, achievable commitments that set the tone for your day. They help you stay present, focused, and aligned with your bigger vision. For instance, in 2015, I launched my first financial service product, a loan program designed to provide accessible funding for small business owners. Every morning, I set the intention *Today, I will approach every challenge with creativity and patience.* This simple act shifted my mindset and helped me stay calm during unexpected hurdles.

And I'm not alone in this practice. Successful entrepreneurs like Arianna Huffington swear by the power of daily intentions.[4] She emphasizes prioritizing well-being in her daily routine, setting intentions like *I will take care of my health first* or *I will be fully present in meetings.*

Try setting an intention each morning. Write it down in a journal or say it aloud to yourself. It can be as simple as *I will listen actively in conversations* or *I will dedicate one hour to deep work without distractions.* Putting your intention into words helps solidify your commitment, and these small daily commitments compound over time and create a foundation for success in your business.

2. Project-Based Intentions

Project-based intentions are linked to specific business activities or milestones. These are the commitments that keep your long-term vision alive while ensuring progress on a tactical level. As CEO of Simplending Financial, my project-based intention was *I will create financial solutions that simplify and empower people's financial journeys.* This intention shaped every aspect of the business, from developing accessible lending options to ensuring transparency and trust with clients.

When Sara Blakely, the founder of Spanx, was developing her first product, she set a clear intention to create comfortable, seamless shapewear that eliminated visible panty lines. This intention guided every decision, from product design to marketing. She wasn't just selling shapewear—she was addressing the frustration many women faced with visible panty lines and uncomfortable undergarments that didn't provide a smooth, flattering fit, and that intention became the driving force behind her billion-dollar brand.[5]

Think about a project you're developing or working on right now. Write it down. What's your ultimate intention for that project? Consider how you want to improve your customers' lives or bring innovation to your industry. A strong intention will serve as your guiding principle, shaping your decisions and keeping you focused.

If you're launching a new business, you might set an intention like *I will build a brand that prioritizes customer experience* or *I will create a product that is both innovative and sustainable.* These clear, guiding intentions will shape your decisions and keep you focused.

3. Life Intentions

Life intentions are broader and often tied to your values and long-term aspirations. These are the guiding principles that help you make decisions and stay aligned with what truly matters. For me, one of my core life intentions is *I will lead with authenticity and integrity in everything I do.* This intention has shaped how I build relationships, run businesses, and even how I navigate challenges.

Oprah Winfrey frequently emphasizes that intention guides her life and choices rather than pursuing external success alone. She has publicly stated that "intention is at the heart of her every decision and has become an intrinsic part of her spiritual journey."[6] This overarching intention has influenced her business ventures, philanthropy, and personal growth. By focusing on *who* she wanted to be rather than *what* she wanted to achieve, she built an empire rooted in authenticity.

Think about what truly matters to you in the long run. Is it financial freedom? Making a difference? Building a legacy? Once you define your life intentions, they become your compass, helping you stay on track even when things get tough.

Setting Your Own Intentions

Intentions aren't about perfection; they're about progress. Some days, your intention might be as simple as *I will show up and do my best*. Other days, it might be tackling a major milestone head-on. The key is consistency—setting intentions, revisiting them, and allowing them to shape your actions.

If you ever feel overwhelmed, start small. Set one clear daily intention and build from there. Trust the process. Every intention, no matter how small, brings you closer to a life and business aligned with your deepest values.

MAKING YOUR INTENTIONS POWERFUL

So, how do you make this work for you? It's simpler than you think. Intentions are not rigid, deadline-driven goals. They are fluid, shaping the way you approach your day, your work, and your decisions. The key is to set them with clarity and purpose.

Make It Meaningful

Intentions work best when they align with what truly matters to you. Instead of setting the intention *I need to be more productive*, try *I intend to bring focus and creativity to my work today*. This shift allows you to guide your actions with purpose rather than pressure. For example, a successful entrepreneur I once worked with ran a design studio. Instead of setting a rigid sales target, she set an intention to serve clients with authenticity and creativity. Within months, she attracted more aligned clients who valued her work, leading to organic growth in her business.

Feel It. Don't Just Say It.

Close your eyes, take a deep breath, and first picture yourself living your intention. See yourself acting, speaking, or working exactly the way you want to show up. Then feel what it's like to embody your intention. Notice how your breathing slows, your shoulders relax, and a sense of clarity settles in. Your brain responds to emotions, so connecting to the feeling makes your intention more powerful.

When I first started my business, I used to set an intention to embrace challenges with confidence. Before an important meeting, I would sit for a minute, breathe deeply, and feel the confidence I intended to bring. This helped shift my mindset from nervousness to self-assurance.

Trust the Process

Intentions aren't about instant results; they're about aligning your thoughts and actions with what truly matters. The real test of trusting the process comes when moments of doubt, setbacks, or success feel out of reach. The truth is, it is easy to stay committed when things are going well, but true resilience is built when challenges arise.

For example, one of my clients wanted to launch a wellness brand. Her first product line was a set of herbal teas designed to help with relaxation and better sleep. When sales were low at the beginning, she felt discouraged and was ready to give up, but I encouraged her to stay true to her intention of helping people live healthier lives.

She took customer feedback seriously, refined the tea blends for better taste and potency, improved her packaging to look more appealing on store shelves, and started sharing practical wellness tips online to build trust with her audience. Over time, she attracted loyal customers who valued her commitment to quality and authenticity. Today, her brand has grown steadily by about 10 percent through word of mouth and repeat buyers who love her products and her mission.

Similarly, in your own business or career, there will be times when progress feels slow, when others may not see your vision, or when challenges make you question whether to keep going. This is when trusting the process matters most. Stay aligned with your intention, keep showing up, and allow time for growth. The results will come.

Write It Down

Putting your intention on paper reinforces it in your mind. Keep a small notebook or use a digital journal to track your daily or weekly intentions.

One of my coaching clients, a busy working mother building her own online brand, uses this practice every day. Each morning, she writes down one simple, clear intention, such as "I intend to prioritize self-care today" or "I intend to communicate openly with my team." She's shared with me how this small habit has transformed her days, helping her feel more balanced, focused, and in control, even during her busiest weeks.

Try this: Revisit your journal or start a fresh page today. Write down an intention for your business or personal growth. A week from now, return to it. How did it shape your decisions and mindset? This simple habit can turn your intentions into tangible progress.

Align Your Environment with Your Intention

Your surroundings influence your mindset. If your intention is to stay calm and focused, curate a workspace that reflects that. A cluttered, disorganized desk can create mental chaos, making it harder to concentrate. If your intention is to foster creativity, surround yourself with inspiring visuals such as artwork, mood boards, or meaningful objects that spark ideas.

When I first started working from home full-time, I noticed how much my environment affected my focus and mood. I used to work at the kitchen table, surrounded by distractions and unfinished chores. It made it hard to stay centered and productive. So, I created a dedicated corner in my bedroom with a simple desk, a comfortable chair, a small plant, and a vision board with images that inspire me. This small change helped me feel more intentional and grounded every time I sat down to work.

Revisit and Adjust

Intentions are flexible. Unlike goals, they are not about hitting a specific target but about how you show up. Revisit your intentions regularly to see if they still resonate.

A friend of mine, a bakery owner, started with the intention to bring joy through food. As her business grew, she adjusted her focus to creating a workplace where employees feel valued. This shift improved both team morale and customer experience.

ALIGNING YOUR ACTIONS WITH WHAT TRULY MATTERS

A meaningful and focused life begins with setting clear intentions. Unlike rigid goals, intentions shape the way you approach your daily actions, ensuring that you align with what truly matters. When you set powerful intentions, you train your mind to recognize opportunities, make better decisions, and stay motivated even when challenges arise.

But intentions alone are just the beginning. To truly bring them to life, you need to create a vivid mental picture of the future you desire. Visualization bridges the gap between intention and reality—it activates your imagination, sharpens your focus, and builds the belief that what you envision is possible. In the next chapter, you will learn how to visualize your future with clarity and purpose, so your intentions aren't just thoughts but the seeds of a future you're actively shaping.

So, what do you intend to do next? Write it down. Commit to it. And watch how it transforms not just your day but your business and your life.

REVIEW QUESTIONS

1. What is my core intention for today? Does this intention align with my values and long-term vision?

2. What are my intentions for a current or an ongoing project?

3. What are my intentions for the life I want to live?

4. How can I better align my workplace with my daily, project, or lifelong intentions?

5. Am I being flexible with my intentions while staying committed to my purpose?

6. How will I track my intentions to stay aligned and focused?

7. How can I reinforce my intention through my actions?

CHAPTER 5

VISUALIZING YOUR FUTURE

*If my mind can conceive it and my heart can
believe it, then I can achieve it.*
—MUHAMMAD ALI

Have you ever felt overwhelmed by the seemingly vast gap between where you are and where you want to be? I certainly have.

It was my first year as a business owner. A steady job had been my safety net, but I had just quit to follow my dream of starting my own lending business. I had high hopes of building something great, making a difference, and becoming financially free. But guess what? I had a lot to do, problems kept arising, and my long list of goals seemed hard to reach.

At one point, the weight of it all felt overwhelming, making it difficult for me to breathe. I was sitting at my desk in my small home office, surrounded by stacks of paperwork and notes. I had so much work to do: calling over fifty potential clients, finalizing the required legal documents, setting up my first proper office meeting, and figuring out how to market my services with almost no budget. I felt paralyzed. It seemed like my goal of securing my first ten clients and generating a steady monthly income was always out of reach, like a distant dream. On one particularly frustrating night at home, I finally gave up after hours of trying to figure out what to do next. The gap between what I envisioned and what I actually had seemed impossible to bridge. I was stuck because I didn't have a clear picture of where I wanted to go. I was so focused on the things that were in my way that I forgot about the goal.

Many of us have had doubts about our skills and ability to succeed at some point in our lives. This may have caused us to avoid opportunities because we were afraid of what might go wrong. When we think about the things we are scared of, the people we shouldn't trust, or the things we don't feel safe about, we are telling our subconscious mind more about our fears. Without a doubt, we are making a clear, negative mental picture of what we are most afraid of, which is why we freeze with fear. In such moments, it's easy to lose motivation.

But we don't have to give in to our doubts and fears. After I had been running my business for about a year, I came across the concept of visualization in a book about personal development. The idea intrigued me right away, but at first, I wasn't sure if it would actually make a difference. But I decided to give it a try, thinking, *What do I have to lose?* I began by closing my eyes, imagining what it would be like to be successful. I imagined what I would be doing, the people I would help, and how free I would feel.

As I thought about this concept, something changed. I could see both the end goal and the paths that would lead me there. It's not enough to just think about your goals; visualization is a strong way to make sure that your actions and thoughts are in line with them. Instead, picture what you want to happen to help you change how you see the present. Make it so clear and vivid that it helps you get where you are going. If you have a clear picture of where you want to go, the next steps will seem less scary and much more doable. These positive thoughts can change the way your mind works so that it stops telling you *I can't* and starts telling you *I already am*.

In this chapter, you'll learn how to use visualization to get from where you are now to where you want to be. I'll also share the tools that have helped me get past feeling stuck and start taking steps toward my goals.

VISUALIZATION IS FOR EVERYONE

Visualization is the art of seeing your desired future as if it already exists. It is the process of making clear mental pictures of what you want to achieve. It is a strong tool that lets you use the amazing power of your subconscious mind. When you keep picturing something, you tell your inner mind to work on making that image come true.

You might believe that visualization is reserved for "dreamers," or those with strong imaginations. Regardless of their artistic aptitude, everyone can learn visualization. You can improve and strengthen your ability to visualize through constant practice. You can still use your other senses and emotions to enhance your visualizations, even if you find it difficult to create clear mental images.

Think of it as a workout for your brain. This method involves visualizing positive outcomes and considering the steps needed to achieve them. However, mastering this requires more than just repeating a daily mantra or maintaining a positive mindset. You can't just visualize and wait for things to magically happen. Visualization techniques go a step further, engaging all five senses and equipping you with practical tools to accomplish actionable tasks.

There is solid evidence that this practice gets your mind and body ready to do what you need to do to reach your goals. You can make your brain work like you are really experiencing your goals by giving your subconscious mind strong pictures and feelings of them coming true.

SCIENCE BEHIND VISUALIZATION

Perhaps you're not entirely convinced, but researchers in neuroscience have been studying the connection between visualization and achievement for years. They've found that imagining ourselves doing something changes the pathways in our brains and creates new links that might help us reach our goals.[1] They've also discovered that using your mind can help you feel better, face your fears, make choices, and reach your goals.

"Imagination is a neurological reality that can impact our brains and bodies in ways that matter for our wellbeing," says Tor Wager, head of the Cognitive and Affective Neuroscience Laboratory at the University of Colorado Boulder.[2] Wager's statement is based on research examining how mental imagery influences brain activity. The study found that when participants visualized positive or calming scenarios, their brains activated regions associated with real-life experiences, including the prefrontal cortex and limbic system, which regulate emotions and stress responses. Notably, those who engaged in regular visualization showed lower stress levels and improved emotional regulation. This suggests that practicing visualization can strengthen mental resilience, enhance focus, and create lasting physiological benefits.

In another study, from 2016, brain scans of people who took part in a twelve-week study on self-guided positive imagery showed that their emotional states, cognitive function, and nonverbal reasoning all got better. Researchers found that positive visualization was linked to more brain activity in areas of the brain that control emotions, empathy, social reasoning, and creative thinking.[3]

Visualization can also help people who are healing from a stroke, dancers who are learning choreography, and professional athletes who are training. The parts of the brain that control movement are stimulated when we imagine doing something. This gets the brain ready to do the action. This mental exercise makes it easier to plan out the steps we need to take to reach our goals.[4]

JOURNALS AND VISION BOARDS

Once you begin to visualize your goals clearly, it helps to capture and reinforce those mental images through tangible tools like journals and vision boards. These are more than just creative outlets—they serve as daily reminders of where you're headed and why it matters.

We've already done some journaling, but let's go a little deeper into how journaling can help you create the business you dream of. A journal allows you to reflect on your aspirations, track your progress, and clarify your thoughts. It can be as simple as writing down what your ideal day looks like, how you want to feel, or the small steps you plan to take. Journaling makes your vision more concrete by putting words to what might otherwise remain a vague feeling. It helps you recognize patterns, stay focused, and remain accountable to your dreams. That's exactly why I encouraged you to keep a journal as you read this book, so you can capture your insights, set clear intentions, and watch your vision unfold page by page.

Vision boards, on the other hand, speak to your visual senses. You can find inspiring images in magazines, online platforms like Pinterest, or by printing photos that resonate with your goals. They are collections of images, words, and symbols that represent the life you want to create. By curating a board that reflects your future, you create a physical representation of your internal goals. Place it somewhere you'll see often—above your desk, beside your bed, or on your phone screen—so that your mind stays engaged with the future you're working toward.

Together, these tools deepen your connection to your desired outcomes. They act as anchors, especially on days when motivation dips. When your energy wanes or doubt creeps in, flipping through your journal entries or glancing at your vision board can reignite your belief in what's possible. They remind you not only of what you want but of who you're becoming in the process.

CLARIFYING YOUR VISUALIZATIONS— A MEDITATION

Before you can fully harness the power of visualization, it's essential to pause and quiet the noise around you. This is not just about picturing a desired outcome—it's about connecting deeply with it. Think of this process as a form of meditation: a moment to center yourself, breathe deeply, and align your thoughts with your deepest desires.

Clarity comes when the mind is calm and focused. In this stillness, your vision becomes more than just a fleeting thought—it transforms into a vivid, emotionally charged experience. Let your imagination flow freely, without pressure or distraction. As you breathe and focus, allow your goals to take shape with greater purpose and intention. This quiet clarity is where true visualization begins.

Create a Quiet Space

Find a calm, distraction-free environment where you can focus. It could be a cozy corner in your home, a library, a study room, or even a peaceful park or garden. Sit comfortably, take a few deep breaths, and relax your mind.

Identify and Visualize Your Goals

Setting goals is the first thing you need to do to start using imagination in your daily life. Write down your short- and long-term goals. Clarify what you want to achieve and why you want to achieve it. If you want to get a promotion, for example, write down the exact job title, the perks of the promotion, and how it will change your life.

Make It Personal

Place yourself at the center of the vision. See yourself succeeding, not someone else. Use affirmations like *I am achieving my goal because I am capable and determined.* An affirmation is a strong way to visualize your goal by telling yourself about it as if you've already reached it. Focus on the good things in this situation and don't think too much about the bad things that might happen. This method for positive visualization is all about making your goals seem like they are attainable.

Use Your Senses

Close your eyes and imagine yourself achieving your goal. Visualize your surroundings: What do you see? Who is with you? What sounds do you hear? Is there music, applause, or the hum of activity? What scents are in the air? Fresh flowers, coffee, or something else? How does it feel? The texture of a handshake, the warmth of sunlight, or the satisfaction of accomplishment? You can really get a feel for the present moment if you use all five senses during your meditation. It will make you want to work hard to make those imaginary times happen in the real world.

Imagine the Journey, Not Just the Outcome

Imagine the specific steps you are taking to reach your goal, ensuring they are achievable and measurable. Visualize overcoming challenges, staying focused, and celebrating small wins along the way. Connect deeply with the emotions you will experience when you achieve your goal. Focus on feelings like pride, joy, relief, or gratitude.

SEE IT, THEN BECOME IT

We've discussed how visualization can be a game-changer in achieving your goals. It has the power to shift your mindset from doubt and fear to belief and action. When you create vivid mental images of your desired outcomes, you train your subconscious to align your thoughts, emotions, and actions with your goals. The connection between visualization and goal setting provides a powerful framework that not only helps you focus but also motivates you to take consistent, deliberate steps toward success.

As we move into the next chapter, keep in mind that visualization is a tool that works hand in hand with planning and perseverance. It's not enough to simply picture your future—you must also actively work toward it.

REVIEW QUESTIONS

1. What is visualization, and how does it differ from setting intentions or goals?

2. How can visualization help overcome limiting beliefs?

3. In what ways has visualization been shown to enhance performance, both in sports and other fields?

4. What are some practical steps you can take to start using visualization in your own life or business?

5. Why is it important to engage all your senses when practicing visualization?

6. What kinds of images, words, or symbols would you like to include on your vision board?

7. Where will you place your vision board so you can see it daily and stay inspired?

CHAPTER 6

SETTING ACHIEVABLE GOALS

Goals are dreams with deadlines.
—NAPOLEON HILL

Do you ever feel like you've set big, beautiful intentions, only to find that your goals seem too far out of reach? Maybe you've told yourself you want to be more mindful or kinder to your team, but when it comes to actually making progress, it feels like you're stuck in quicksand. You know what you want, but it seems so abstract— how do you even begin turning that vision into something actionable?

You are not alone. A lot of entrepreneurs struggle with this very thing: setting intentions that feel meaningful but not knowing how to move forward in a tangible way. You're caught in the cycle of excitement and motivation, but without concrete steps, the end result feels elusive, and the pressure to achieve feels overwhelming.

I have been there too. When I first started my lending business, I was full of big dreams—being a more present leader, working smarter, building a strong company culture. But I kept feeling frustrated. The goals I set were so broad, so abstract, that they didn't feel possible to actually achieve. I'd start strong but then get lost in the day-to-day chaos, only to find that my intentions were left hanging, with no real plan to bring them to life.

Then, about two years into my lending business, one afternoon, I was sitting at my desk, scrolling through my email, when an article from a leadership blog popped up in my inbox. The headline read: "Goal Setting: Turning Dreams into Achievable Plans." I was intrigued, so I clicked on it, not expecting much. But as I read through the article, something shifted. The author shared a simple framework for breaking down big goals into small, actionable steps. She emphasized the importance of making goals specific, measurable, and time-bound—something that was completely missing from my approach.[1]

It felt like a light bulb turning on in my head. I suddenly realized that I'd been treating my dreams like they were tasks on a to-do list instead of actual objectives that needed a real plan to execute. It wasn't enough to want to be a better leader or to build a stronger culture. I needed concrete actions, not just broad intentions.

That was my aha moment. I understood then that setting achievable goals was the bridge between intention and action. It's about turning your big-picture aspirations into small, manageable steps that push you forward. So instead of just "being more mindful" or "improving communication," I started to create a plan with clear actions like "dedicate ten minutes every morning to mindfulness meditation" or "set up a weekly meeting to improve team collaboration."

In this chapter, you'll learn how to transform those abstract, lofty intentions into concrete, attainable goals that you can actually achieve. We'll talk about setting SMART goals—specific, measurable, achievable, relevant, and time-bound—that give you the structure and direction you need. Plus, we'll explore how to break down those goals into bite-sized actions that build momentum, day by day.

GOALS KEEP US MOVING FORWARD

Do you feel like you have great intentions but struggle to make real progress?

Many entrepreneurs, especially women, unknowingly hold themselves back by not being specific about what they want and how they are going to achieve it. It's easy to fall into the trap of playing small, holding ourselves back, and missing the opportunities that could truly move us forward. Over time, these small actions—or lack thereof—accumulate and begin to chip away at our self-esteem. The belief in our own skills diminishes, and eventually, we're left feeling stagnant and unsure of why we're not progressing, yet unable to pinpoint the cause.

I've been there myself. In the early years of my entrepreneurial journey, I'd convince myself that I was working hard, but the results didn't match up. I'd spend days answering emails, tweaking my website, and brainstorming new ideas. But the tasks that would've really moved the needle—like making key sales calls, refining my pitch, or setting up strategic partnerships—kept getting pushed to the side because they felt overwhelming. In the end, I was left wondering why my business wasn't growing as fast as I'd hoped.

The truth is, without clear goals, it's easy to stay stuck. Many people mistakenly believe that they're making progress toward their objectives, but in reality, they're just spinning their wheels. A little procrastination here, a bit of avoidance there, and the most important tasks—those that would truly push them toward growth—get brushed aside because "there's just not enough time."

When you set clear goals, you identify what you want to achieve and establish measurable and specific objectives to achieve it. This can include creating long-term goals and short-term goals that help you focus on your objectives, track your progress, and attain your desired result. They are the desired outcome you or your team are committed to achieving within a specific time frame.

The key here is taking what feels overwhelming and turning it into something practical and within reach. Instead of feeling like you're chasing an ever-moving target, we are going to create a game plan that puts you in control of your success.

WHY WE NEED TO SET GOALS FOR OUR ENTREPRENEURIAL JOURNEY

As entrepreneurs, we're constantly navigating uncertainty. And in the early stages of building a business, it's easy to get swept up in passion and ideas. You may know what kind of leader you want to be or the kind of company culture you hope to create, but without clearly defined goals, it's all too easy to lose momentum in the busyness of daily operations. But when you set goals—especially ones that are specific, measurable, and time-bound—you turn uncertainty into direction. Your goals help you make better decisions, allocate resources wisely, and prioritize what really matters.

Setting goals is a necessity for any entrepreneur who wants to grow with direction and purpose. Goals provide structure. They act as signposts on the road, helping you track your progress and stay aligned with your vision. They give clarity when things feel chaotic, and they keep you anchored when you're faced with setbacks or distractions.

More importantly, goals fuel accountability. When you write down a clear objective, you create something you can return to and measure against. It becomes easier to course correct, adjust your strategy, or celebrate your wins. And when your team knows where you're headed, they can rally behind the vision and take purposeful action too.

In short, goals help you move forward with intention. They're the difference between being busy and being effective. Without them, you risk working hard without making meaningful progress.

SCIENCE BEHIND GOAL SETTING

Research in psychology and neuroscience has shown that setting clear goals brings immense power into our mindsets and emotional states. Clear goals involve the activation of specific brain regions generally involved in motivation, goal-directed behavior, and self-regulation, enabling one to maintain focus, overcome adversities, and develop resilience.[2]

In an earlier study, in 2001, experts in Great Britain started working with 248 people for two weeks to help them get into better exercise habits.[3] The people were split into three groups. Those in the first group were the "control" group. They were only told to keep track of how often they worked out.

The "motivation" group was the second one. They were told to keep track of their workouts and read some materials about how exercise can help them. People in the group were also told how exercise could lower the risk of coronary heart disease and make the heart healthier.

The third group was the final one. They received the same talk as the second group, which left them equally motivated. However, they were also asked to make a specific plan for where and when they would work out the following week. Every person in the third group wrote the following sentence: "I will do at least twenty minutes of vigorous exercise on [DAY] at [TIME] in [PLACE] over the next week." All three groups left after receiving these directions.

The surprising outcome revealed a compelling truth: 35–38 percent of people in the first and second groups worked out at least once a week. (It was interesting that the motivational talk given to the second group didn't seem to change their behavior in an effective way.) But more than twice as many people in the third group—91 percent—worked out at least once a week.

People in Group 3 were much more likely to actually work out if they wrote down a plan that included exactly when and where they were going to do it.

It may have been even more surprising that having a clear plan worked so well, even without strong motivation. The number of exercises completed by Group 1 (the control group) and Group 2 (the motivation group) was pretty much the same. Another way to say this is that the researchers found that "motivation had no significant effects on exercise behavior."

This contrasts with how most people talk about change and goal achievement, often using words like *drive, determination,* and *desire.* The truth is that we all have some of these qualities. If you want to make a change, there's already some "desire" within you.

Researchers found that your plan for action, not your amount of motivation, is what makes you act on that desire.

ALIGNING OUR GOALS AND ACTIONS

Here's the hard truth: Behaviors must change in order for your actions to be fully in line with your goals. If you continue to avoid the tough but important tasks, your actions won't support your belief in your ability to succeed. And without that belief, it's hard to see growth.

I've seen this time and time again in my own business and in the journeys of other successful female entrepreneurs. Take, for example, Jessica, a fellow entrepreneur who runs a successful online boutique that sells handmade jewelry and accessories. For months, she kept pushing aside the most important task on her list—reaching out to suppliers that could help her scale. She felt that it was too much work and that she didn't have enough time to handle it. But when she finally decided to tackle that task head-on, her business grew by over 25 percent, and the opportunities she'd been waiting for started pouring in.

The key here is simple: To succeed, you need to ensure that your actions align with your goals. That means you have to be intentional. Ask yourself: *What am I avoiding? What's the one thing I could do today that would move me closer to my goal?* Once you identify those critical actions and take them, you'll be amazed at how quickly things start to shift.

If you're still stuck, it might be time to revisit your goals and align your actions with them. When you make a conscious effort to match your behavior with your aspirations, you'll begin to see real progress, and your self-esteem will grow as a result. You'll stop wondering why you haven't reached your growth targets, and you'll start taking the steps necessary to get there.

THE POWER OF SMART BUSINESS GOALS

So, after identifying the goals that truly align with your vision, how can you set these goals for yourself and actually stick to them?

As a businesswoman, I have learned firsthand that you need more than just big ideas to succeed; you need a plan. And not just any plan but a plan that's concrete, measurable, and, most importantly, achievable. This is where SMART goals come in.

If you've never used the SMART goal framework before, trust me, it will change the way you approach everything, from your business strategy to your personal goals.

SMART stands for specific, measurable, achievable, relevant, and time-bound. Let's break it down:

Specific

Your goal needs to be clear and well-defined. Instead of "I want to grow my business," make it specific: "I want to increase my online sales by 15 percent in the next quarter." This specificity gives you a target to hit and allows you to focus on the *what* and *why* behind your goal.

A few years ago, I set a specific goal to increase my online sales by 20 percent in the next quarter. Instead of just saying "I want to grow my business," I focused on actionable steps: refining my website for better conversions, launching a targeted email campaign, and collaborating with influencers. This clarity gave me a measurable target and kept me focused. By the end of the quarter, I achieved the 20 percent increase and gained valuable insights into my customers. Being specific with goals turned vague ideas into clear, impactful actions that drove real results for my business.

Measurable

You need a way to track progress and know when you've reached your goal. That means using numbers, percentages, or milestones to measure success. For example, rather than setting a vague goal like "improve customer engagement," you might say, "I want to get five hundred new followers on Instagram and increase engagement by 30 percent this month."

A business coaching client of mine once wanted to boost their social media presence, so we set a measurable goal: Increase Instagram followers by five thousand and engagement by 20 percent in one month. We tracked progress weekly using analytics tools and adjusted strategies, like posting more interactive content. By month's end, they hit both targets, with an increase in followers and engagement. Having clear numbers allowed us to stay focused and pivot when needed, ensuring we were always on track to achieve the goal. This measurable approach made success feel attainable and motivated them to keep pushing forward.

Achievable

Your goal should be realistic. I get it: We all want to scale our businesses to the moon, but shooting for the stars without a clear path could leave you frustrated. I've had to remind myself (and my clients) that it's better to set a goal that challenges you but is within your reach.

For example, I once helped a client in retail set an achievable goal: Instead of aiming to double their revenue in one month, we targeted a 10 percent increase. We focused on boosting sales through targeted promotions and refining their customer service. By the end of the month, they not only hit the 10 percent increase but felt motivated to keep refining their strategy. The realistic target kept them on track, and the success gave them the confidence to set bigger, more challenging goals for the future, showing that steady, manageable growth is just as rewarding as fast growth.

Relevant

Make sure your goal aligns with your larger vision. For instance, Melanie Perkins, cofounder of Canva, set a relevant goal to simplify design for everyday people, aligning with her vision of democratizing design. Early in her journey, she focused on making the platform easy to use for non-designers, which directly supported her broader goal of empowering individuals to create professional-looking designs. Instead of getting sidetracked by nonessential features, Perkins's team relentlessly focused on user experience. This focus helped Canva grow rapidly, attracting millions of users and becoming one of the most successful tech companies, with a valuation of over $40 billion.[4] Every goal kept her vision at the forefront.

Time-Bound

Every goal needs a deadline. Without it, procrastination creeps in, and you end up wondering where the time went. When Kendra Scott, the founder of Kendra Scott Jewelry, began her business in 2002, she launched with just $500 and worked out of her spare bedroom in Austin, Texas. At the time, she was navigating financial constraints and raising a young child, yet she remained deeply committed to turning her vision into reality.[5] By moving forward decisively and staying focused despite limited resources, Scott built steady momentum in the early days of her company. That persistence and follow-through ultimately helped her grow the brand into a multimillion-dollar business with a nationwide presence.

HOW BETTY TRANSFORMED HER FASHION BRAND WITH SMART GOALS

Let me share a story of one of my clients, Betty, who used these principles to successfully grow her business. Betty, an entrepreneur in the fashion industry, came to me feeling overwhelmed. She wanted to grow her brand but didn't know where to start. We sat down, defined her specific goal (to increase sales by 20 percent in six months), and applied the SMART framework to her plan.

She measured progress by tracking online sales each month. The goal was achievable because it was based on data and trends in her market. Betty's goal was relevant to her broader objective of expanding her brand, and we set a time-bound deadline for her six-month target.

Then, we broke it down further into manageable tasks. One of her key strategies was to collaborate with influencers. So, we mapped out a timeline:

- Month 1: Identify five influencers in her niche.
- Month 2: Reach out and schedule partnerships.
- Month 3: Launch the first influencer campaign.

> By breaking her goal into steps, Betty avoided burnout and kept focused on actions that directly contributed to her target. And guess what? She exceeded her goal, increasing sales by 25 percent in less than six months.

WHEN YOUR GOALS FEEL TOO LARGE

You've set your SMART goals, but how do you avoid feeling overwhelmed when you look at the larger picture? You break them down into smaller, bite-sized actions that you can tackle day by day.

For example, when I first launched my company, my goal was to increase sales by 25 percent within six months. That seemed huge, but I broke it down into smaller, manageable steps:

- Week 1: Update the website with new products and launch a social media campaign.

- Week 2: Email existing customers with a special offer.

- Week 3: Host a webinar to engage with potential customers.

- Week 4: Evaluate results and adjust strategy.

Each action built on the next, creating momentum, and before I knew it, I was making a steady 5 percent month-over-month growth in sales. Breaking it down like this makes the journey feel less intimidating and more like a series of small victories that add up over time.

Using the SMART framework, set a date for your goal, like "I will launch my new product by the end of Q2," and then create smaller milestones to hit along the way.

TURNING DREAMS INTO ACHIEVABLE MILESTONES

The secret to turning lofty intentions into achievable goals lies in clarity, structure, and consistent action. When you break down your goals into smaller steps, they become less overwhelming, and you'll find yourself celebrating small wins along the way.

As you set your goals, take a moment to reflect on your "why." What drives you? What does success look like to you? Once you have that clarity, use the SMART framework to map out a realistic path to success. Whether it's scaling your business, launching a new product, or increasing your network, you can use these same tools to make it happen.

Ready to turn those big dreams into achievable goals? Let's dive in and get started. The world is waiting for what you have to offer, and it all starts with clarity and commitment to the journey ahead.

REVIEW QUESTIONS

1. What is the main challenge many entrepreneurs face when setting goals?

2. According to the research study in Great Britain, what was the key factor that led to increased exercise participation among the third group?

3. What are some common ways people unknowingly hold themselves back from achieving their goals?

4. How did Jessica, the entrepreneur mentioned in the chapter, overcome her hesitation and scale her business?

5. Explain the SMART goal framework and why each component is important in setting achievable goals.

6. Why is aligning daily actions with long-term goals crucial for success, and how can one ensure this alignment?

ACTIVITY: SET YOUR OWN SMART GOAL

1. Think of one major goal you want to accomplish in your business.

2. Write it down in its current form.

3. Now, refine your goal using the SMART framework:

    - Specific: How can you make your goal clearer and more defined?

    - Measurable: What metrics or indicators will you use to track your progress?

    - Attainable: Is this goal realistic based on your current time, resources, and abilities? If not, how can you adjust it?

    - Relevant: Why does this goal matter for your business right now?

    - Time-bound: By when do you want to accomplish this goal?

4. Break your SMART goal into three to five smaller, actionable steps.

5. List them in order of priority or sequence.

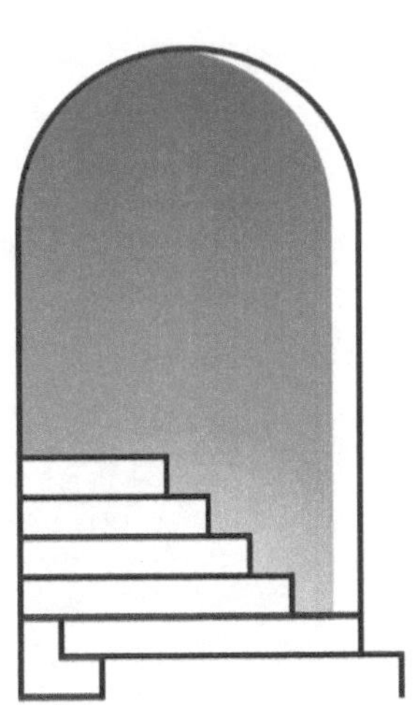

SHE BELIEVES:

BELIEVING FULLY IN YOURSELF AND YOUR BUSINESS

CHAPTER 7

COMMITTING TO YOUR VISION

Commitment is what transforms a promise into reality.
—ABRAHAM LINCOLN

When Leah first came to me for business coaching, she was on the edge of quitting.

She had launched her small business six months earlier with a bold vision: to create a sustainable fashion brand that prioritized both ethics and elegance. At first, it felt like everything was falling into place. Her brand gained early traction, her social media presence grew, and she received enthusiastic feedback from customers. But when a key supplier failed to deliver, two launches fell through, and her savings began to dwindle, she started to question everything.

"I don't think I'm cut out for this," she said to me during one of our coaching calls. "Maybe I was naive to think I could pull this off."

Leah didn't have a vision problem; she had a commitment problem. Instead of pivoting or finding new solutions when her supplier issues arose, she froze. She delayed making hard decisions, postponed new marketing plans, and spent weeks second-guessing herself rather than moving forward. She kept waiting for a sign—more money in the bank, a perfect partnership, or someone to reassure her she was on the right track.

But I reminded her: Leadership begins with self-leadership. When you're the visionary, you are also the one responsible for holding the line when no one else sees the finish line. Your team, your clients, your community—they all take their cues from how you show up.

This is what I want to talk to you about in this chapter.

It is exhilarating to have a vision. It motivates you, floods your mind with possibilities, and stirs belief that you're meant to build something meaningful. But what happens when the excitement fades? What happens when the fear creeps in, the progress slows, or life throws unexpected setbacks your way?

This is where many people stumble. They stumble in staying devoted when the dream starts demanding more than they expected.

Maybe you've been there. Maybe you're there right now. Maybe you've set ambitious goals before, only to pause when the obstacles multiplied. Or you've shown up, worked hard, and wondered why your breakthrough hasn't arrived yet. It's frustrating. It's exhausting. And it's all part of the journey.

Because the truth is that commitment isn't convenient. It requires showing up when you'd rather quit. Believing when results are delayed. Choosing discipline over distraction. It means leading yourself even when you're tired, even when others don't get it, even when progress feels invisible.

In this chapter, I'll show you how to make a decision so solid it anchors you, even on the toughest days. You'll learn how to lead from within, embody your vision with consistency, and turn your commitment into a nonnegotiable.

Because the gap between those who talk about success and those who live it isn't talent or luck—it's commitment. And when you commit fully, you don't just chase a vision; you become the leader who brings it to life.

Let's get to work.

RETURNING TO YOUR VISUALIZATIONS

There will be days when your vision feels distant, when motivation dips, and life pulls you in unexpected directions. In those moments, come back to the vision board you created. Your visualization isn't a nice idea to think about when things are calm; it's a foundation. It reminds you of what matters, where you're going, and why you started.

When challenges come, your vision becomes a stabilizer. It keeps your focus sharp and your heart aligned with purpose. This is where leadership begins—with your ability to lead yourself. True leadership means holding steady when things shake around you. It means carrying your intention into action, even when the path ahead isn't clear.

Each time you revisit your visualization, you strengthen your direction. You remind yourself that what you see in your mind is worth the effort it takes to build in real life. You reawaken belief. You regain energy. You stay grounded in purpose.

This is how you build commitment—not when things are easy but when you choose to move forward anyway.

ALIGNING YOUR PASSION, PURPOSE, VISION, AND GOALS

As you commit to your vision, it's essential to recognize that your initial visualizations and goals might need refinement to stay true to your evolving passion and purpose. Visualizing your future is not a one-time event—it's a dynamic process that grows as you gain clarity about what truly drives you.

When you lead yourself and others, your vision must resonate deeply with your core values and ignite your passion. This alignment fuels your perseverance and inspires those who follow your leadership. If your goals or mental images feel disconnected from what excites and motivates you, it's time to adjust them. Ask yourself: *Are these goals serving my true purpose? Does my vision energize me and align with the impact I want to make?*

Adjusting your visualizations means refining the picture in your mind so it reflects your authentic ambitions and the legacy you want to create. It might mean shifting focus from outcomes that once seemed appealing but no longer feel meaningful, to new goals that align with your purpose. This kind of leadership starts with your self-awareness and honesty. You must be willing to pivot, even if it means letting go of previous plans that no longer serve your growth or the greater good.

By consistently realigning your goals and visualizations with your passion, you strengthen your commitment and lead with conviction. This clarity enables you to inspire others, because you lead from a place of authenticity, demonstrating that true leadership is rooted in purpose-driven action. Your ability to adjust and stay aligned will ensure your vision remains vibrant, achievable, and impactful—even through challenges.

STAYING COMMITTED WHEN THINGS GET DIFFICULT

There will be moments on your journey when everything seems to fall apart, when the plan you were sure would work crumbles, when people you trusted walk away, or when life throws you a storm you never saw coming.

These moments don't mean your vision is invalid; they mean you're human and that you're being tested to see how committed you really are.

You may have visualized a thriving business, and now you're staring at declining sales and mounting bills. Maybe you've taken bold steps toward a leadership role, only to face rejection or get passed over again. Perhaps you've launched your dream project; poured in time, money, and heart; and it just isn't gaining traction. Or maybe your personal life is in chaos—a health issue, a broken relationship, a loss—pulling your focus away from your goals.

When these things happen, it's tempting to give in to the fear that you're not cut out for this. That your vision was too big. That maybe you were wrong to believe.

But here's the truth: Your ability to keep going when things go wrong is what builds your legacy. Real leaders aren't shaped by moments of ease; they're forged in adversity. Leadership is about standing in the fire, still choosing your vision, still showing up when you have every excuse not to.

You must ask yourself in these moments: *Do I believe in my vision enough to recommit to it, even now?*

A few years into starting my own business, it took a hit I didn't see coming. A deal I'd counted on fell through at the last minute, and it left me scrambling to pay suppliers. I felt humiliated. I started questioning everything. But then I sat with myself and asked, *What would the version of me who's already succeeded do here?* And I found a way forward. I renegotiated timelines, I reached out for help, I shifted strategies—but I did not abandon the vision.

This is what commitment looks like.

When things go wrong, you don't abandon the dream; you go back to your vision. You reconnect with your "why." You revise the plan, adjust your methods, but you hold the line on your purpose.

If you're in a moment right now where nothing seems to be going right, I want you to pause and remind yourself: Storms pass. Struggles shape you. But only if you don't quit.

You don't have to pretend it's easy. But you do have to decide that it's worth it. And if it's worth it, then it's worth fighting for, no matter what.

Developing Resilience

Resilience is the ability to bounce back and grow stronger after facing difficulties or failures. It isn't something you either have or don't have; it's a discipline you practice. And one of the most effective ways to strengthen it is by learning how to reset after a setback rather than pushing through blindly. When things go wrong, don't pretend it didn't hurt. Acknowledge the disappointment, then pause—not to quit but to recalibrate. Let's look at a few ways we can build our resilience when we're feeling challenged:

- Build in structured recovery time. Just as athletes schedule rest days to allow their muscles to rebuild, you need to give yourself room to mentally and emotionally recover after stress or failure. This might mean taking a weekend away from constant productivity to reflect in silence, to be near nature, or to nourish your creative side. Stillness, when used wisely, isn't laziness— it's strategic restoration.

- Reframe how you interpret resistance. When something feels difficult or uncomfortable, instead of seeing it as a red flag, start asking yourself: *Is this discomfort a sign of growth?* More often than not, resistance shows up when you're moving into unfamiliar territory—not failing but stretching. That shift in perception gives you the endurance to keep going when others stop.

- Keep a long-term perspective. Train yourself to zoom out. Will this challenge still matter in five years? Or even in five weeks? When you learn to differentiate between real threats and passing storms, you gain emotional control. Not everything deserves your energy or anxiety. Resilience thrives when you keep your eyes on your larger mission.

Above all, your story gains power every time you get back up. People aren't drawn to those who've never fallen—they're inspired by those who refuse to stay down. Your scars become your strength when you stop hiding them and begin seeing them as proof of your survival. You don't build resilience overnight. But each time you choose to show up—with your heart still open and your vision intact—you're training yourself to rise stronger than before.

Staying Agile and Flexible

If you've ever clung tightly to a strategy that's no longer working, you know how quickly rigidity can turn into burnout.

When your plans unravel or the path ahead becomes unclear, your success depends on your agility—that is, your ability to adjust without losing your purpose. Agility is more than quick reaction; it's strategic adaptation. It's the skill of holding your vision firmly while allowing the methods to shift.

Agility also shows up in how you listen—to your team, your clients, and yourself. When you pay attention to the signs around you, you spot opportunities for innovation that a fixed mindset would miss. You begin to lead not only with confidence but with curiosity. You learn to course correct without shame.

The most effective business owners know how to pivot. They ask:

What's still in my control? What options haven't I considered yet? You stay empowered by focusing on action over anxiety. And this requires flexibility in addition to agility.

At the core of flexibility is the belief that progress is rarely linear. You might need to take a detour, slow your pace, or try something unconventional. That doesn't mean you've failed; it means you're committed enough to find a way, even if it's not the one you originally imagined. Being flexible doesn't mean abandoning your dreams; it means being wise enough to evolve your approach when reality changes.

By being both agile and flexible, you can grow into your vision, not by forcing every detail to match your plan, but by learning to respond with wisdom, creativity, and courage when the plan changes. That is what positions you as a leader—not in perfect execution but in unwavering commitment to the outcome, no matter what route it takes to get there.

Reframing Failures as Feedback

The most successful people don't see setbacks as signs to quit; they see them as lessons. Every time you face a challenge, ask yourself: *What is this teaching me? How can I use this to grow?* The faster you embrace this mindset, the stronger your belief will become.

A great example is Brian Chesky, the cofounder of Airbnb. In the early days, Airbnb struggled so badly that Chesky and his partners couldn't pay their rent and almost shut the company down. To keep the lights on, they sold novelty cereal boxes and used that money to fund their idea a little longer. When their original model didn't gain traction, they pivoted how they marketed Airbnb, focused on high-quality photos and trust-building tools, and repositioned the platform as an affordable travel experience for everyone.[1] That shift not only saved the company but turned it into one of the most successful start-ups in the world. Chesky's ability to see setbacks as feedback instead of failure turned near bankruptcy into a billion-dollar business.

COMMIT TO YOURSELF WITH THE "NO MATTER WHAT" CONTRACT

True commitment means deciding, once and for all, that giving up is not an option. It means making a promise to yourself that you'll stay the course—even when your plans unravel, even when the results don't come quickly, and especially when the pressure feels unbearable.

One of the most powerful ways to solidify that decision is by creating a written contract with yourself: a "No Matter What" contract. This becomes your anchor—something to return to when discouragement creeps in, when fear gets loud, and when quitting feels like the easier path.

I know this works because I've relied on it in a deeply personal way. A few months after Simplending Financial had launched, I took a bold risk and invested in an online platform that promised to scale our client outreach. I paid for the highest-tier service up front, and it was a huge chunk of our operating budget at the time. Within six weeks, it was clear we had been misled. The system was clunky, the leads were unqualified, and support was nonexistent. I was furious with myself. I remember sitting in my car outside our tiny office space wondering how I'd tell my team that I'd wasted the money.

I wanted to pull back, play it safe, shut down anything that looked remotely like risk. But that morning, I opened my notebook and found the "No Matter What" contract I had written before launching the business. It wasn't filled with lofty phrases or motivational quotes; it was practical and personal. I had listed exactly what I believed in, what I was building, and the values I had committed to uphold regardless of outcomes. I had signed it, dated it, and even written a short paragraph to my future self, reminding her that setbacks didn't have the power to define the mission.

Reading that contract didn't erase the mistake, but it shifted how I responded to it. Instead of spiraling into shame or fear, I owned the error, gathered my team, explained what went wrong, and invited them into the rebuild. That experience didn't destroy Simplending—it matured it. We became smarter, more united, and clearer about our processes. And that clarity helped us double our revenue the following quarter.

You don't need to wait for a disaster to write your own contract. In fact, it's best to do it now, before you're in crisis. Write down what you believe in, what you're building, and what you're unwilling to walk away from. Be specific. Make it real. Then sign it. That document won't make you immune to failure, but it will make sure failure doesn't have the final say.

HOW I USE MY "NO MATTER WHAT" CONTRACT

I keep my contract where I can see it often—taped inside the first page of my journal and pinned to a corkboard in my home office. On especially tough days, when client payments are delayed, when plans don't go as expected, or when I start doubting whether I have what it takes to lead, I read it out loud. I treat it like a mirror that reflects who I said I would be before fear and frustration crept in. It grounds me in my "why" and reminds me that this journey isn't about perfection; it's about persistence.

There was a time when I almost didn't launch a key financial literacy workshop. I had only four sign-ups with three days left. My instinct said to cancel. But the contract I wrote reminded me that impact isn't always measured by numbers, especially not at the beginning. I went ahead with those four people, and two of them became long-term clients who referred others. That experience taught me not to trust my emotions in the moment but rather to trust the commitment I had already made to show up, serve, and stay the course.

Your "No Matter What" Contract

Here's a version of the contract I use. Feel free to adapt it, print it, and keep it somewhere visible. Read it when you're tempted to give up, and let it remind you who you chose to be.

"NO MATTER WHAT" CONTRACT

Date: _________________________

I, ________________, commit to my vision of ___________________

____.

I understand that challenges will come. I may face rejection, doubt, confusion, and even failure. But I am making a decision today to hold on to what I'm building, no matter what.

I promise to show up even when I feel discouraged.

I promise to keep learning, growing, and leading with integrity.

I promise not to shrink when things get hard but to rise with resilience.

I will remind myself why I started.

I will not abandon my calling because of temporary discomfort.

I will pivot when needed, rest when necessary. But I will not quit.

This vision was planted in me for a reason. And I choose to honor it with my commitment.

continued

Signature: _______________________________

Vision statement (in your own words):

____

____

____

____

Top three values I will lead with:

1. ____

2. ____

3. ____

Who I'm becoming through this journey:

____

____

____

WHEN YOU STOP WAVERING, YOU START WINNING

Your journey will have ups and downs. There will be moments when doubt creeps in, moments when things don't go as planned. But when you refuse to waver, when you stay committed no matter what—that's when your vision turns into reality. Commitment creates certainty. And certainty creates results.

So, ask yourself: *How deeply am I committed to my dreams?* Because the moment you decide to go all in, everything starts falling into place.

REVIEW QUESTIONS

1. What makes it difficult to stay committed to your vision when things go wrong?

2. How does acting in alignment with your future self help you stay committed?

3. Why is it necessary to revisit and refine your vision regularly instead of relying on your initial plan?

4. In what ways can you adjust your goals and visualizations to stay aligned with your passion and purpose?

5. What is the link between clarity of vision and your ability to lead with confidence?

6. What specific habits can help you build resilience during hard seasons?

7. Why are agility and flexibility crucial when your original plans fall apart?

8. How can setbacks and failures be reframed as valuable feedback?

9. How does writing a "No Matter What" contract help reinforce your long-term commitment?

10. How can you lead yourself and others with consistency, even when motivation fades?

CHAPTER 8

CONFRONTING OUR LIMITING BELIEFS

You begin to fly when you let go of self-limiting beliefs and allow your mind and aspirations to rise to greater heights.
—BRIAN TRACY

vividly remember attending my first National Private Lending Association (NPLA) meeting. As I entered the room filled with industry professionals, seasoned veterans, and experts from across the country, the familiar and heavy doubt set in: *Do I belong here?* I looked around and noticed very few women, fewer still who looked like me or shared my background. Instantly, the voice of insecurity crept up, reminding me of how out of place I felt in my first college accounting class, where I was one of only a handful of women.

At that moment, I had two choices: Let the thought consume me or challenge it. I chose to ask myself a different question: *Why wouldn't I belong here?* After all, I had earned my place in that room. I had built a company, worked with investors nationwide, and gained a valuable perspective to share. With that shift, I began to feel less like an impostor and more like someone who had something unique to offer.

This was the beginning of recognizing my limiting beliefs and learning to spin them into positive affirmations. Remember in Chapter 3 when we explored how developing a growth mindset allows us to reframe challenges as opportunities? That same mindset is crucial when facing limiting beliefs. We must believe we're capable of evolving beyond them.

Limiting beliefs are deeply ingrained thoughts or perceptions that constrain us from reaching our full potential. This is where a growth mindset becomes foundational. When we accept that abilities and intelligence can develop with effort, it becomes easier to challenge these ingrained beliefs. These beliefs are often formed during childhood, influenced by societal norms, past experiences, or fear of failure. However, research in neuroscience, psychology, and behavioral science reveals that these beliefs are not fixed and can be reprogrammed.

In this chapter, you'll uncover what limiting beliefs really are, where they come from, and how they quietly shape your choices and confidence. You'll see how these hidden thoughts can hold you back from your full potential and, more importantly, how to break free from them.

IDENTIFYING YOUR LIMITING BELIEFS

Before you can change a limiting belief, you have to name it. It sounds simple, but most of us carry these invisible thoughts for so long that they feel like facts, not beliefs. The first step is to bring them into the light.

1. Pinpoint where you feel stuck or held back. Maybe it's in your business, your finances, your confidence to pitch an idea, or your belief that you can lead a team.

2. Listen for the quiet story your mind tells you: thoughts like *I'm not smart enough for that*, *I always mess things up*, or *People like me don't do things like this*.

3. Write down what you discover. Seeing it on paper makes it real and easier to challenge.

4. Challenge each belief. Ask: Who told me this? Is it really true? What evidence do I have that says otherwise?

5. Shine a light on it, question it, and get ready to rewrite the story for good. You might be surprised to realize that what you've accepted as truth is just an old fear wearing a new mask.

This simple awareness is powerful. You can't reframe what you can't see. Start here and take back control.

SCIENCE BEHIND LIMITING BELIEFS

Before we can change our limiting beliefs, we should understand why we have them in the first place.

As you probably guessed, our limiting beliefs are shaped in the brain, primarily in the amygdala. This part of the brain, at the top of the brain stem, is responsible for emotional responses like fear, often reinforcing limiting beliefs as a protective mechanism.[1] It helped our ancestors survive thousands of years ago by inducing a fight-or-flight reaction in the event of actual danger, such as a predator, a storm, or a circumstance where survival was at stake. But today, that same system misfires, treating emotional risks—like launching a business, making an investment, or putting ourselves out there—as if they were actual physical threats.

The amygdala releases a barrage of stress hormones when fear takes over, making us acutely aware of every potential negative outcome. The worst-case scenarios are what our brains focus on and make us believe are unavoidable. Limiting beliefs originate from there. We begin to think that we lack the necessary skills, that we are not competent enough, or that we cannot take that risk. We unconsciously search for proof to support our ideas because the brain prefers to be correct, which perpetuates a vicious cycle that holds us in place.

But we aren't controlled only by our amygdala. The prefrontal cortex, at the front of the brain just above our eyebrows, responsible for rational thought and decision-making, plays a key role. We can harness the power of our prefrontal cortex to reevaluate and modify beliefs about our personal abilities, skills, and potential for success.

The brain is a highly adaptable organ, capable of change through a process called *neuroplasticity*. This concept, extensively researched by Dr. Michael Merzenich, shows that neural pathways are not static but can be reshaped based on new experiences and thoughts. Limiting beliefs are formed through repeated neural connections, and by actively challenging these beliefs, we can create new, empowering pathways.[2] This is exactly what a growth mindset nurtures: the understanding that our brains can adapt, our thoughts can shift, and we can rise beyond the boundaries we once believed were fixed.

In addition, research by Dr. Joseph LeDoux suggests that understanding and consciously managing emotional triggers can help rewire our responses to self-limiting thoughts.[3]

As entrepreneurs, we have the power to rewire our thinking and break free from limiting beliefs. When we actively challenge negative thought patterns and leverage the brain's neuroplasticity, we can reshape our mindset for success. When we are able to understand our emotional triggers, it helps us make bold, confident decisions, because growth starts with the beliefs we choose to embrace!

In Chapter 3, we discussed how shifting to a growth mindset involves engaging the rational part of our brain to question our assumptions and take bold steps. That same practice empowers us here, as we move from reactive fear to intentional growth.

HARNESSING FEAR FOR SUCCESS

Fear has a cunning way of manipulating us. It doesn't always manifest as paralysis or panic; occasionally, it disguises itself as logic, whispering all the reasons why something won't work, why you're not ready, or why it's safer to remain in your current position, when in fact we are merely holding ourselves back. It deceives us into believing that we are protecting ourselves.

For entrepreneurs, fear is ever present. All decisions are plagued by the dread of failure: What if this investment is a failure? What happens if I make a mistake? Then there's the worry of being rejected—what if I present my idea and nobody finds it appealing? Strangely enough, there's also the dread of success—what if I do this? What if expansion results in increased demands, accountability, and expectations?

Fear often stands between you and the action you know you need to take. It doesn't always announce itself loudly. Sometimes, it shows up as hesitation, self-doubt, or constant overthinking. You start questioning whether you're qualified enough, ready enough, or deserving of the opportunity in front of you. You hesitate. Not because you lack ability but because you want certainty. You want to know the outcome before making the move.

But comfort is not conducive to growth, and growth rarely gives you guarantees. It asks for courage first.

The truth is that fear is not the adversary. In actuality, it is evidence that we are leaving our comfort zone and venturing into new areas. The secret is to change our perception of fear. Instead of interpreting it as a stop sign, we might begin to see it as an indication that something significant is about to happen. Every successful leader, investor, and entrepreneur has been afraid at some time or another. They moved forward not because they'd overcome it but because they acted in spite of it.

When we learn to harness our fear rather than run from it, everything changes. Being afraid of failing shows that we are invested in the project. Rejection serves as a reminder that we are taking risks. Fear of being successful? That's merely a sign that we are becoming more advanced.

Fear will never go away. So, the next time fear attempts to stop you, don't ask yourself, *What if I fail?* Ask yourself instead, *What if I don't even try?* Will you let fear drive, or will you take the wheel?

USING FEAR TO BUILD BELIEF AND TRUST IN YOURSELF

When you're unsure, belief becomes your turning point. It's the inner conviction that your experience, preparation, and values are enough. Belief pushes you forward, even when you're uncomfortable. It helps you make the call, send the pitch, walk into the meeting—because deep down, you know what you bring to the table.

Still, belief isn't always steady. That's when trust comes in. Trust that your efforts matter. Trust that your journey is worth the risk. You don't have to wait until you're fearless. You just have to choose to move, even while the fear is still there.

The shift happens when you ask better questions—not *What if I fail?* but *What if I succeed?* Not *Am I ready?* but *Am I willing to try?*

The moment you begin to trust yourself—fully and without needing proof—is the moment you start stepping into the future you've imagined.

CONFRONTING IMPOSTOR SYNDROME

I will always remember the day I closed my first big deal. I had been striving for this kind of opportunity for years. It was evidence that all of my hard work, calculated risks, and unwavering determination had paid off. But rather than rejoicing, I was overcome with some disturbing thoughts: *What if I don't deserve this? What happens if they find out I'm not as capable as they believe?*

That was the full force of impostor syndrome.

Impostor syndrome, according to psychologists, is the persistent conviction that one's achievement is unmerited and the product of luck rather than skill. People who suffer from impostor syndrome feel like "frauds" and are always afraid of being discovered, regardless of how much evidence there is to support their ability. Dr. Pauline Clance and Dr. Suzanne Imes, who first identified the phenomenon, found that high achievers are often the most susceptible. Entrepreneurs, in particular, are prime targets.[4]

Building something from the ground up—be it a financial portfolio, a brand, or a business—may come with a lot of responsibilities. There is no boss to approve your work, and there is no road map. You, your goal, and the urge to realize it are all that are involved. The fear of making a poor decision might exacerbate self-doubt in sectors such as private lending, where transactions entail substantial sums and investor confidence.

However, the truth is that impostor syndrome is really a mental trick, a warped perception of reality that makes competent people feel inadequate. Since the brain creates neural pathways based on recurring ideas, as I mentioned earlier, if you tell yourself repeatedly that you're not as skilled or accomplished as you are and don't deserve success, your brain will reinforce that notion. Thankfully, the contrary is also true: You can rewire your brain to accept your success rather than doubt it by purposefully changing your viewpoint.

Here are some strategies to overcome impostor syndrome:

- **Redefine success.** Many entrepreneurs hold themselves to impossible standards because they feel that they are not deserving of their accomplishments unless they are specialists in every facet of their company. However, growth is more important for success than competence. Pay attention to what you're learning rather than what you don't know.

- **Find a mentor.** Making connections with seasoned experts in your field not only yields insightful information but also serves as a reminder that nobody is an expert in everything. Every prosperous businessperson has experienced periods of uncertainty. Speaking with people who have been in your position before will help you understand that feeling like an impostor does not imply that you are one.

- **Keep track of your accomplishments.** The survival mechanism that once helped our ancestors avoid danger is now a source of self-doubt since the human brain is programmed to remember failures more vividly than victories. This bias can be mitigated by documenting achievements, such as closed agreements, client endorsements, or revenue milestones. Looking back on concrete evidence of accomplishment can be a potent remedy for impostor syndrome.

The truth is, impostor syndrome never completely goes away. Your previous doubts will try to resurface as you advance in your career. However, confidence is about not letting that feeling control your behavior, not about never feeling like an impostor. Remember, the next time you start doubting whether you belong, remind yourself: You wouldn't have made it this far if you didn't. And the fact that you care so much about getting it right? That's proof that you do.

SILENCING THE INNER CRITIC

Just when I thought I had mastered overcoming these limiting beliefs, I was faced with a new challenge that stirred them all up again. After several years of running my company, I was invited to be a guest on RCN Capital's podcast, a prominent platform in the lending industry. The invitation was a huge honor and a significant milestone in my career. But as soon as I accepted, those old thoughts crept back: *Am I really the best person for this? What if I stumble? What if people think I don't know what I'm talking about?*

Even though I had battled similar thoughts before, this felt different. It was a new level of exposure and validation, which brought with it heightened insecurities. But instead of letting the doubts paralyze me, I remembered the tools I had already developed. I took a moment to breathe and reflect on my journey, reminding myself that I had been invited because of my expertise and unique perspective. I told myself, *I am more than prepared for this. I will share my insights confidently and authentically.*

When the day came for the podcast, I walked into the studio with nerves, yes, but also with a deep sense of calm. I had transformed my thoughts into a powerful affirmation that carried me through the conversation, and afterward, I felt the triumph of not only sharing my knowledge but also silencing my inner critic.

REWRITING YOUR STORY

The truth is, limiting beliefs never entirely go away, especially as you continue to grow and evolve in your career. With each new threshold you reach, those old insecurities will try to resurface. But you don't have to let them win. Instead, you can face them head-on, armed with the knowledge that you are capable, deserving, and prepared.

For me, this journey has been about more than just silencing doubts; it's been about learning to trust myself. Every time I've entered a new room, whether at an NPLA meeting or in front of a podcast microphone, I've reminded myself of my worth and embraced the process of turning those limiting beliefs into affirmations of strength.

Remember: You *do* belong in the rooms you enter and deserve the opportunities you're given and the successes you achieve. Fear and limiting beliefs will try to tell you otherwise, but they don't get to write your story. You do. And that's what I want for you.

So instead of asking, *What if I'm not good enough?* start asking, *What if I am?* Because the moment you choose to believe in yourself, everything starts to change.

REVIEW QUESTIONS

1. What is the first step in overcoming limiting beliefs, and why is it important?

2. In what ways does fear contribute to limiting beliefs, and how can entrepreneurs reframe their perception of fear to use it as a tool for growth?

3. Why is courage more important than certainty when overcoming doubt or fear?

4. How can impostor syndrome affect entrepreneurs?

5. What are some strategies used to combat impostor syndrome, and how can these strategies be applied to other areas of life?

6. Describe how reframing limiting beliefs into positive affirmations helped the author manage insecurities.

7. Can you think of a time when reframing your own thoughts could have been beneficial?

8. How do you confront your limiting beliefs, especially when they resurface at new levels of success?

9. What is one practical step you can take this week to challenge a limiting belief you've been carrying?

CHAPTER 9

BUILDING UNSHAKABLE BELIEF

In 2022, I was working with a client who ran a small but growing construction business. For years, he had taken on minor home renovation projects—kitchen remodels, fence installations, driveway repairs. But now, he was ready to take a leap. He had landed a contract to lead his first multiunit residential remodel, which was a major step up in scope, responsibility, and risk.

He needed funding to hire extra hands, rent heavy equipment, and secure materials in advance. The opportunity was there. His team was ready. And he brought me in to help secure the loan.

At first, it looked promising. We submitted all the necessary paperwork, the lender seemed cooperative, and we were hopeful for a quick turnaround. But then the hurdles came. The lender raised new concerns about my client's lack of prior experience with projects of that scale. Requests for revised budgets and tighter timelines started pouring in. Underwriters questioned every line item. Weeks passed, and my client grew more discouraged with each delay. He even considered walking away from the contract and sticking to the smaller jobs he was used to.

I'll admit I felt the pressure, too. There were times when I wondered if we were trying to force something that simply wasn't going to happen. But somewhere deep inside, I knew we couldn't stop now. We restructured the loan request, reworked the proposal to strengthen his case, and pressed forward with new urgency.

Eventually, the funding was approved.

That single deal helped my client complete the project and transformed his business. Within a year, he was taking on even larger developments, hiring more workers, and bidding confidently for contracts he once thought were out of reach.

Looking back, it wasn't the numbers that made the difference; it was belief. When the pressure mounted, what pushed us through wasn't certainty—it was the refusal to quit.

In this chapter, you'll learn what it takes to develop that kind of belief—the kind that shows up when the plan doesn't. You'll understand how belief builds on your thinking, fuels your resilience, and creates the inner foundation for breakthrough results.

CONNECTING BELIEF AND YOUR GROWTH MINDSET

Before you can fully embrace belief, it's important to understand the mindset that makes belief possible.

Remember, a growth mindset means believing that your abilities and intelligence can improve through effort, persistence, and learning. It's the difference between *I'm just not good at this* and *I can get better if I keep trying*. For example, maybe you've struggled with public speaking, launching your business, or setting boundaries. A fixed mindset says, *I'm not a speaker* or *I'm not cut out for this*, but a growth mindset says, *I'm still learning, and every step forward counts*.

When you operate from this mindset, you start to see failures as feedback and obstacles as opportunities—not as signs that you're not good enough. If a pitch gets rejected or a deal falls through, instead of walking away, you ask, *What can I improve for next time?*

This mindset prepares you to move from passive hope to active belief. Instead of waiting to feel confident, you take action—trusting that clarity and confidence will come through experience. It shifts your focus from proving yourself to improving yourself. You stop needing everyone else's approval and start recognizing your own growth.

As we now move into the deeper work of belief, remember this: Your thoughts are the foundation—but belief gives them life. Without belief, even the most powerful thoughts stay locked in theory. With belief, they move you to act. Belief is where the transformation begins.

MOVING BEYOND THINKING INTO BELIEVING

Many people stop at thinking. They analyze, plan, and dream. They say things like *I think I can do this* or *I think this might work out.* But belief takes it a step further. Belief says, *I'm committed. I'm in. I trust that this is possible—even when I don't have proof yet.*

Thinking is passive. Believing is active.

Thinking happens in your mind. Believing shows up in your actions.

You can think your way into hesitation; you can't believe your way into inaction. When you believe, you move, even if you're unsure. Even if it's uncomfortable. Even if it doesn't make perfect sense yet.

The transition from thinking to believing is where transformation begins. It's the moment you stop waiting for certainty and start walking in courage.

So, if you're stuck right now—overthinking, hesitating, holding back—ask yourself: *Do I believe, or am I just thinking?*

Because belief is what turns possibility into progress.

DEFINING FAITH AND BELIEF

As you move from simply thinking to actively believing, it helps to understand how belief and faith work together yet differ, with each playing a unique role in how you pursue your goals. Belief and faith are two important qualities that propel achievement, particularly in the realm of entrepreneurship. While they are frequently used interchangeably, I'd like to explain their definitions in the context of this book.

Belief is founded on conviction. It is a deep belief that something is feasible, that your vision is attainable, and that your efforts will be fruitful. It is what motivates an entrepreneur to invest in a firm before seeing a single dollar of return. A young woman beginning a boutique consulting firm may not have a full client roster yet, but she is confident in her experience, networking skills, and the value she delivers to the market.

Belief is based on information, experience, and personal trust in your talents. A seasoned financial advisor will not hesitate to offer a long-term investing strategy if he believes the historical data supports it. A baker introducing a new product line is confident that years of developing recipes and researching client preferences will result in success.

When you truly believe, you operate from a position of certainty—not because you see the outcomes right away but because you believe in the process and your ability to make things happen.

However, faith goes one step further. Faith is steadfast trust in the unseen, confidence in results that have yet to be realized. The entrepreneur perseveres in the face of numerous rejections, believing that the right opportunity will arise at the right moment. The artist continues to paint, hoping that their work will one day be recognized, even if no one is buying.

Faith serves as a bridge between our efforts and the unknown, providing certainty that even when circumstances appear uncertain, a road ahead exists. A single mother working persistently to establish her business while raising children may not experience instant success, but she believes that her sacrifices will be rewarded. A first-time author pouring their heart into a manuscript without a publisher in mind continues forward with faith, hoping that the perfect audience will find their writings. Faith keeps us going when rationality tells us to quit, circumstances suggest it's impossible, and terror takes over.

Many people equate faith with religion or spirituality, and while faith can have a profound spiritual dimension, it is not restricted to religious views. In this book, faith refers to an unwavering belief in the process—whether that belief is anchored in God, the universe, or the conviction that endurance will eventually lead to achievement.

As a female entrepreneur in the financial world, faith in myself has served as my anchor. It has required me to trust that my hard work, resilience, and honesty will lead to success, even in the face of doubt. When conviction alone feels insufficient, faith is what propels us ahead. It is the power that converts belief into action, enabling us to persevere, innovate, and lead with purpose.

$3 MILLION LOAN STORY

In December of 2023, my team and I were assisting a client who was developing eight ground-up duplex homes that would total up to over $3 million in loan amount, our largest loan yet. Our client had a strong plan, a reliable contractor, and a clear vision. My role was to assist him in securing the necessary funding to bring the initiative to life.

At first, everything appeared to be heading in the right direction. The application process was started, and we were optimistic. But then we encountered difficulties: approval delays from the lender, changing requirements from the underwriters, uncertain loan conditions

continued

that kept shifting based on market risk assessments, and constant back-and-forth conversations where our client was losing patience. Delays kept happening, and I truly wondered if the transaction would ever go through. The customer became increasingly concerned, and I began to wonder whether I was wasting my time on something that was simply not meant to happen.

I was on the edge of stepping back and urging my client to consider other possibilities. But something inside me refused to give up. I revised my plan, polished our approach, and pushed fiercely for approval. Finally, on the last day of the year, the deal was cleared to close, and we funded Simplending Financial's largest deal size to date!

Looking back, I can see how simple it would have been to give up when things didn't go as planned. However, faith is more than just believing when things are going well; it is also about pushing forward when everyone urges you to stop. Trusting the process is acting despite uncertainty, confident that persistence will always yield results.

A TOOL TO STRENGTHEN YOUR BELIEF: THE EVIDENCE JOURNAL

It takes time to develop belief in yourself and faith in your abilities. I've been able to help myself on this journey with something I call the "Evidence Journal," which I've found to be one of the most effective instruments for quickening that process. By compiling evidence of your success, no matter how tiny, this notebook helps you drown out self-doubt.

Consider it a bank of confidence: You make a deposit each time you accomplish a goal, overcome an obstacle, or get good feedback. These deposits build up over time, providing indisputable evidence of your ability, growth, and potential for success.

How to Use It

At the end of each day, take a few minutes to write down at least one piece of evidence that supports your growth. It could be

- A task you completed despite initial hesitation

- A positive comment from a client, boss, or peer

- A problem you solved with creativity or resilience

- A risk you took, even if it felt uncomfortable

- A moment you felt proud of yourself

It doesn't have to be monumental; small wins matter. Maybe you spoke up in a meeting when you usually stay quiet. Maybe you took the first step toward a new goal.

Be sure to record each of these wins in your Evidence Journal. They're proof that you're making progress.

Next time self-doubt creeps in, flip through your journal. You'll quickly realize you are stronger than you think.

Converting Limiting Beliefs to Positive Affirmations

The first step to overcoming limiting beliefs is becoming aware of them. Often, these beliefs are deeply ingrained, born out of past experiences or societal expectations. For a long time, I didn't even realize how much my internal dialogue was holding me back. Thoughts like *I'm not good enough* or *I don't deserve to be here* seemed like facts, not beliefs. I became acutely aware of how much my internal dialogue was holding me back. These kinds of thoughts once dominated my mind, especially when stepping into new roles or opportunities.

To break this cycle, I had to get intentional about spotting them, using these methods:

- I pinpointed where I felt stuck—in business, finances, or self-confidence.

- I paid attention to the quiet story my mind whispered when I faced a big opportunity.

- I wrote those thoughts down so I could see them clearly and challenge them head-on.

But awareness is not enough. The real work comes in reframing those thoughts into something positive. Instead of *I don't belong here*, I began to tell myself, *I'm here for a reason; I have value to contribute*. The more I repeated these affirmations, the easier it became to believe them.

Each time I reached a new threshold in my career, whether it was securing a larger loan or landing a bigger deal, those limiting beliefs would rear their head again. It was like hitting a new level in a video game, with harder challenges and a tougher boss to defeat. I realized that success didn't mean the absence of doubt; it meant learning to manage it. Each time I felt those familiar insecurities creep up, I repeated my affirmations: "I deserve to be here. I'm capable. I'm ready for this challenge."

Surrounding Yourself with Belief Builders

The people you spend time with will either reinforce your beliefs or undermine them. If you're constantly around people who doubt your dreams, it will be harder to maintain your conviction. Surround yourself with those who see your potential, remind you of your worth, and push you to aim higher.

As a young business owner, I sought out a mentor who had established a successful business from the ground up and could teach me how. She understood what I was going through—she had had questions and doubted everything she did. But she was stronger now, and she saw qualities in me that I didn't always see in myself. Her encouragement, counsel, and belief in my abilities inspired me to believe in myself even more. When I failed, she said that failure was part of the process. She reminded me of my previous victories when I didn't believe in myself. The fact that someone believed in me made all the difference.

If you are finding it difficult to believe in yourself, ask yourself: *Who am I surrounded with? Do they uplift me or keep me down?* Spend time with people who inspire you to dream bigger, not with people who make you doubt yourself.

FIND THE RIGHT PEOPLE— IN PERSON OR ONLINE

If you're not currently surrounded by belief builders, don't worry. You can find them. Start by identifying where people with similar goals or values gather. This could be local meetups, workshops, networking events, professional associations, or community classes.

If in-person meetings aren't feasible, look online. Join social media communities, virtual masterminds, or online groups where encouragement and personal development are prioritized. Platforms like LinkedIn, Facebook groups, or coaching forums can offer consistent support and insight. Follow leaders, authors, or mentors who align with your vision— listen to their podcasts, read their books, engage with their content.

Look for people who not only inspire you but challenge you. The right people won't let you settle. They'll stretch you.

Nurture Relationships with Your Belief Builders

Once you've found belief builders, the key is to nurture those relationships intentionally. Here's how:

- **Be consistent:** Check in regularly. Send a quick message, schedule monthly catch-ups, or join weekly study or accountability groups.

- **Give as much as you receive:** Don't just seek encouragement—offer it. Celebrate their wins, listen deeply, and pray for them. Mutual investment strengthens the bond.

- **Be vulnerable:** Share your doubts honestly. This opens the door for deeper trust and meaningful support.

- **Stay rooted in your values:** As you grow, make sure your relationships are anchored in shared faith and integrity. Choose connection over convenience.

The people who walk with you on your journey can become the very pillars that hold you up when you feel like giving in. Invest in those relationships.

THE TURNING POINT IS BELIEF

When I look back, I can say with certainty that belief, not strategy or hard work, was the most important thing that changed my direction. You can learn new things, change the way you do things, and get past problems, but if you don't believe in yourself or your vision, none of it will stick. People notice when you believe in yourself no matter what. As your actions line up and your attitude changes, doors start to open in ways you didn't expect.

Now, think for a moment: What do you think would happen if you decided right now that you can do it? That you are worthy? Do you believe you can do it?

What if you didn't hold back but instead moved forward as if you were already successful? What would be a different way for you to deal with problems? Are you willing to risk more?

Unshakable belief isn't about ignoring your fears or acting like you won't fail. Having a strong belief that you will be successful no matter what is important.

The world has to agree with you once you believe it.

REVIEW QUESTIONS

1. Why is belief considered more powerful than talent, intelligence, or resources in achieving success?

2. What role does mindset play in the transition from thinking to believing?

3. How does the chapter define belief in relation to proof and success?

4. Why is taking action before feeling ready important in building belief, according to the author's experience?

5. What is the purpose of the Evidence Journal, and how does it help strengthen belief over time?

6. How can self-doubt be reframed as a sign of growth rather than failure?

7. How can belief influence the way you present yourself to the world?

8. What practical steps does the author suggest for strengthening belief over time?

PART 3

SHE ACTS:
GOAL SETTING WITH PASSION AND BELIEF

CHAPTER 10

ACTING WITH PASSION TO GROW YOUR BUSINESS

The path to success is to take massive, determined action.
—TONY ROBBINS

We've already discussed how embracing your passion boosts motivation, brings clarity, and helps you identify what truly excites you, especially in the early stages of building a business. But passion is more than just what you do; it's about how you show up every single day, especially when things get hard.

If you are truly passionate about your business, it should be seen in more than just your products or marketing. It should shape the values you live by, the way you build relationships, and how you treat your customers. Whether you're a solo entrepreneur or you lead a team, the way you establish and grow connections should reflect the passion and purpose that fuel your business. This is the heartbeat that keeps you and your team focused, no matter what challenges come your way.

I once worked with a client, Judith, who had a hair care business. She was genuinely committed to helping Black women appreciate their natural hair by developing products that nourished and strengthened it. When she first started, she was ecstatic to share her knowledge, establish her brand, and make a difference.

But months later, she came to me, absolutely exhausted. Sales were slow, competition was fierce, and she felt like she was putting everything into her business for little return. "I don't know if I have what it takes," she said. "I still love what I do, but I don't feel the fire anymore."

I asked her a single question: "Why did you start?"

She paused. Then, gradually, she began to speak about her vision— how she wanted to empower people to embrace their natural hair, how she had tried for years to find the proper products, and how she had once been excited to wake up and share her knowledge with others. Somewhere along the line, she had begun to focus solely on the difficulties and lost sight of the passion that had originally motivated her.

So, we made a change. Instead of viewing passion solely as an emotion, I helped her see it as a commitment. She reconnected with her "why" and adjusted her daily practices by setting intentional routines: starting each morning by reviewing her "why" written on a sticky note above her desk, reconnecting with past customer testimonials for motivation, and dedicating blocks of time each day to creating fresh content that reflected her personal story and mission. We also developed a system where she reached out to five potential customers or collaborators daily, regardless of how she felt. This shift from emotion-driven action to purpose-driven discipline helped her stay grounded, especially on the tough days.

Within a few months, everything changed. Her enthusiasm returned, she began engaging more with her consumers, and her business began to grow not just because of strategy but because people could see the love behind her brand. Most significantly, she discovered joy in her work again.

That is what this chapter is about. We're not just talking about what excites you; we're talking about how to channel that passion, use it to overcome obstacles, and make it the driving force behind your success.

In this chapter, you'll discover how to move beyond simply feeling passionate about your business to truly acting on that passion every day. You'll learn why passion must be visible in your daily habits, your relationships, and the way you serve your customers, and how to keep that spark alive when challenges and doubt creep in.

It's time to turn passion into action—because belief is powerful, but what you do with it is what matters. Let's go!

USING PASSION TO GROW YOUR BUSINESS

Passion is the lifeblood of any successful business. It's what keeps you going when things get tough, what sets your business apart, and what draws others to your products or services. But here's the truth: Passion isn't sufficient. You must understand how to harness it, guide it, and translate it into tangible results.

You are not alone if you have ever been enthused about your own business idea but unsure how to transform that excitement into something practical. Many entrepreneurs begin with passion, only to become trapped when faced with hurdles. The trick is to understand how to use your passion as a motivator rather than just a feeling. Let's look at it in more detail.

Translate Passion into Daily Actions

Consider this: Anyone can be enthused about something new and fresh. But what happens months later when the enthusiasm has worn off and you're stuck repeating the same mundane tasks? That is where genuine passion is tested. It doesn't matter how loudly you express your dream; what matters is how continuously you work for it.

Passion is demonstrated by how you show up every day, even when no one is looking. It is not all about huge, flashy moments. It's not simply about beginning your company with enthusiasm, announcing it to the world, or reaching huge milestones.

When I first founded Simplending Financial, I had a great vision of creating a lending business that didn't merely approve or deny applications but also empowered people with financial solutions tailored to their specific requirements. I intended to help small company owners, first-time homebuyers, and families who had been passed over by traditional banks get fair, honest, and individualized financial assistance.

I believed we could create something that was about more than just numbers and credit scores but also about empowering individuals to take charge of their financial futures. I envisioned a company where clients were more than just applications on a computer but actual individuals with meaningful ambitions, challenges, and stories. However, simply having a vision was insufficient.

It wasn't just about saying, "We care about our clients." Every interaction had to reflect that concern. Every underwriter review, meeting, and customer communication was an opportunity to demonstrate our devotion through action.

Did it become exhausting? Of course. There were days when I felt like I was drowning in paperwork, resolving customer difficulties, and making difficult decisions. But I reminded myself that passion isn't about always being excited; it's about choosing to care, even on difficult days.

Your customers, clients, and team members can tell how much you care—not only in huge marketing initiatives but in the nuances. Running a café entails more than simply pouring coffee; you must also remember your regulars' names and how they take their drinks. If you sell handcrafted things, it's more than simply earning sales; it's about taking the time to properly package each order, including a thank-you card, and ensuring that every product is of high quality. If you're a coach or consultant, it's not just about what you teach; it's also about actively listening, providing specific advice, and making each client feel appreciated.

People notice when you put your heart and soul into even the smallest tasks. And when they notice, they believe you.

Turning Routine into Purpose

It's easy to get caught up in the daily grind and see tasks as just stuff to do. But when you adjust your perspective and start viewing everything as a building block toward your vision, everything changes. At the end of the day, your success isn't determined by one big moment of inspiration. It is based on what you do every day, repeatedly. Instead of seeing sales and spending as mere required business tasks, approach them as opportunities to better understand and enhance your business. Treat email responses as opportunities to establish loyalty and relationships. Utilize social media to inspire and engage with your audience.

When you infuse purpose into your daily tasks, even the routine becomes meaningful. Purpose-driven routines help you stay focused, fuel your passion, and make every small action count toward your bigger vision. So take a fresh look at your day-to-day activities: Organize your time, prioritize what matters most, and build habits that move you closer to the business—and the life—you want.

Aligning Your Company Values with Your Actions

While culture is internal, your values are external—what your customers experience and associate with your brand. These are the guiding principles that shape your messaging, marketing, and customer interactions. They give your brand identity and meaning beyond what you sell.

For example, if you run a real estate business, don't just sell homes—sell a vision of community, security, and possibility. Show your passion by offering personalized home-buying experiences, hosting neighborhood tours that highlight the area's lifestyle, or creating educational resources that empower first-time buyers. By going beyond transactions and focusing on meaningful connections, you establish a culture that resonates with clients and keeps them coming back.

Your company should be passionate not only about what it sells but also about the experiences it creates.

Consider asking yourself the following questions: How do I want my consumers and staff to perceive my brand? What values do I want my company to represent?

To help clarify your company's core values, consider using the following table. These examples can inspire you to define what truly matters in your business and how you want to be known by both your team and your customers.

CORE VALUE	YOUR VALUE IN ACTION
Integrity	Always delivering on promises and being transparent with customers
Innovation	Embracing new ideas and staying ahead of trends in your industry
Customer-Centricity	Designing experiences around customer needs and feedback
Community	Giving back, partnering locally, or supporting causes that matter to you
Sustainability	Reducing environmental impact and promoting ethical practices
Excellence	Holding high standards for quality, service, and results
Accountability	Owning your outcomes—good or bad—and learning from them

Choose three to five values that align with both your personal passion and your business mission. These will help guide your decisions, shape your brand identity, and build trust with your audience.

Transform Passion into a Magnetic Brand Identity

Your company is about more than just selling a product or service; it's about generating an emotional experience for your customers. And that experience starts with your branding. If you're truly passionate about your work, that passion should shine through every aspect of your business: your visuals, messaging, customer service, and overall brand vibe.

Think about the brands you're naturally drawn to. They likely have a clear personality, a message that speaks directly to you, and a presence that's instantly recognizable. Take Apple, for example. Their sleek, minimal branding reflects their core values of simplicity, innovation, and ease of use. Every interaction with their brand reinforces who they are and what they stand for.

Now imagine a small boutique candle company. They hand pour each product, use earthy tones and handwritten labels, and pair it all with messaging that evokes warmth, calm, and sustainability. Before you even light the candle, you already feel something. That emotional resonance is no accident. It's passion turned into brand identity.

That's exactly what you want to create.

A magnetic brand identity connects your passion to your audience's emotions. It helps people not only understand what you do but feel why you do it. When your passion is visible and consistent, your business becomes memorable—and meaningful.

For instance, if you run a hair care business, your brand can be a direct reflection of your values. If you believe in self-love, authenticity, and empowerment, let that shape your entire customer experience. Use bold, uplifting visuals and messaging that celebrate individuality. Offer products for a range of hair types and styles, and share tutorials that help customers embrace their unique beauty. Highlight real people through testimonials, transformations, and inclusive campaigns. When your brand expresses what you truly care about, it becomes more than a business—it becomes a movement.

PRACTICAL STRATEGIES FOR PASSION IN ACTION

Embrace Imperfection and Take the First Step

One of the biggest barriers to discovering and pursuing your passion is fear—fear of failing, being judged, or even succeeding. Often, we hesitate to follow what excites us because we worry about what others will think or doubt our own abilities. But here's something to remember: You don't have to be fearless to move forward; you just have to be willing to try.

Take Janice Bryant Howroyd, founder and CEO of ACT-1 Group, the largest minority woman–owned employment agency in the United States. She started her business with just $1,500 and faced massive uncertainty. As a young Black woman entering a competitive corporate world, she encountered fear and self-doubt. But instead of waiting until she felt completely ready, Howroyd chose to move forward anyway—trusting her vision and learning as she went. Her willingness to start before she felt "perfect" led her to build a billion-dollar company.[1]

Here's the truth: No one begins as an expert. Passion doesn't require perfection—it requires movement. The more you take action, the more confidence you'll build. The goal isn't to be flawless; it's to begin.

Doubt is natural. What matters is how you respond to it. Surround yourself with people who uplift and support your growth. Seek mentors who've walked a similar path. And remind yourself that pursuing what matters to you is worth the risk.

You don't need to have it all figured out. You just need to take the next right step.

Try Different Things and Act

Consider Jane. She's in her second year of undergraduate studies and absolutely loves animals. Volunteering at a local shelter fills her with joy and purpose. Yet she's majoring in computer science, which she doesn't enjoy, simply because it promises a stable career. Imagine if Jane allowed herself to explore a path that aligned with her passion—perhaps switching majors to animal science or starting a blog on pet wellness. Taking small steps like these could open the door to a future filled with more fulfillment and impact.

Many people feel stuck not because they lack passion but because they overthink it. They wait for a perfect plan or the "right time" and end up never taking meaningful steps forward. But clarity comes through action, not perfection.

That's where experimentation comes in. Passion rarely starts as a loud calling. It often begins as a quiet curiosity. The more you engage, the clearer it becomes. Trying, failing, adjusting, and trying again is often the only way forward.

You don't need to overhaul your entire life to begin. Start small: Take a weekend class, volunteer for a cause you care about, or begin a side project. Explore what makes you feel energized and alive.

And don't be afraid to evolve. Passions change as we grow. The goal is not to have it all figured out but to stay curious, open, and willing to explore. Remember, passion thrives not in planning alone but in motion. This is a journey—not a destination.

Keep Learning All the Time

Passion thrives when you're committed to continuous growth and learning. It's not just about doing what you love—it's about diving deeper, expanding your skills, and pushing your boundaries. Every new thing you learn feeds your passion, making it stronger and more meaningful.

Consider Mary Barra, who made history as the first female CEO of a major global automaker—General Motors. She began her career at GM as a co-op student, inspecting fenders, and steadily rose through the ranks by embracing every opportunity to learn. From engineering to business strategy, Barra committed herself to lifelong learning, adapting to industry shifts and leading with vision and resilience. Her journey reflects how passion, combined with a drive to keep growing, can lead to extraordinary impact.[2]

You don't need to aim for world-changing innovations, though. Read books, attend workshops, listen to podcasts, or network with others in your field of interest. Every bit of knowledge adds fuel to your passion's fire. The more you grow, the clearer your sense of purpose becomes.

Reflect and Reassess Regularly

Passion isn't static—it evolves with you. Life changes, and so can your interests. Regular reflection helps you stay aligned with what truly excites you. Set aside time to ask yourself: *Is this still bringing me joy? Am I growing? Does this still feel meaningful?*

By checking in with yourself, you'll stay connected to your authentic desires and be ready to pivot when needed. Remember, passion is a journey, not a destination.

USING PASSION AS A MOTIVATOR

Passion is a core motivator that sustains effort over time, even when things get tough. Unlike external motivators like money or praise, passion comes from within. It energizes, focuses, and pushes you to persevere, even through failure, fear, and fatigue. But not all passion is equally helpful. When harnessed well, passion fuels grit, resilience, and purpose. When left unchecked, it can lead to burnout or obsessive striving. The ability to channel passion keeps you going and positions you to lead by example. People are drawn to those who stay the course with clarity and conviction.

In this section, you'll learn how passion functions as a powerful motivator and how you can tap into it to remain committed, focused, and energized during life's most challenging seasons. And as you learn to sustain that motivation, you'll naturally step into roles where others look to you for direction and inspiration.

Reignite Your Passion Regularly

There will be times when you feel exhausted or uninspired, no matter how driven you are. In order to continue going forward, even when things become difficult, it is imperative that you actively rekindle your enthusiasm.

- **Reconnect with your "why."** Your purpose is the foundation of your passion. When times get tough, remind yourself why you started in the first place. Revisit your initial vision and the goals that excited you in the beginning.

- **Surround yourself with inspiration.** Stay connected to mentors, read books, listen to podcasts, and engage with people who fuel your drive. Listening to stories of people who've been through what you're going through can give you the boost you need.

- **Take breaks to recharge.** Passion fades when you burn out. It's important to step away when needed, so you can return with fresh energy. Taking time to rest doesn't mean you're losing momentum—it means you're refueling for the next stage of the journey.

Use Passion to Push Through Fear

Passion stands out as a powerful remedy for fear because it shifts your focus from what could go wrong to what matters most. When you deeply care about something, your desire to pursue it becomes stronger than the fear of failing. Passion narrows your attention to your mission and fuels a sense of purpose that drowns out self-doubt. Instead of being paralyzed by fear, you're energized by the drive to make an impact, and that determination pushes fear into the background. This is the essence of true leadership—choosing to act in spite of fear. True leaders are driven by conviction, not applause.

I remember the first time I had to pitch my company's vision to a group of potential investors. It was a room full of seasoned financiers: sharp, analytical, and visibly skeptical. My hands were slightly trembling as I clicked through my slides, and part of me wanted to rush through it and get it over with. I wasn't sure if they'd understand my vision or see the value in what I was building.

But then, I shifted my focus. I stopped worrying about how they saw me and started thinking about why I was there in the first place. I believed in the mission. I wanted to create financial access for people who had always been overlooked. I was tired of watching communities get left behind. That passion, my "why," cut through the noise of fear and grounded me.

I spoke from the heart. I didn't have all the polish, but I had conviction. That moment taught me something invaluable: When you lead with purpose, people feel it. Even if they don't agree with everything you say, they remember how you made them feel. That's the mark of a leader: someone who inspires others by standing firm in their purpose, even in uncertainty.

That presentation reminded me that purpose is more powerful than perfection. When you're rooted in passion, confidence grows. You don't need to know everything. You just need to care deeply enough to keep showing up. And the more you show up with passion, the more others will follow your lead, even if they're afraid too.

Stay Committed Even When Motivation Fades

Commitment is what keeps you going, even when motivation wanes. Your dreams become reality when you fuel your dedication with passion.

Commitment is what keeps you moving forward, even when motivation begins to fade. Your dreams become reality when you fuel your dedication with passion. One powerful way to sustain your commitment is by developing a regular routine that supports your passion—taking small, consistent steps that help you stay on course, even on the days when you are fighting with resistance. It's also essential to keep your final objective in sight. Create a mental or physical road map to your desired destination, and remind yourself of that end goal whenever the journey feels challenging. Finally, surround yourself with people who believe in you. The right support system can make all the difference when discouragement creeps in, helping you rise back up and continue toward your dream.

Finding Meaning in the Struggles

Challenges are inevitable, but passion is what keeps you in the game. It's what turns struggles into stepping stones, fear into motivation, and setbacks into comebacks. By reigniting your passion regularly, pushing through fear, turning setbacks into lessons, and fueling your passion with purpose, you create an unstoppable drive that will carry you through even the toughest moments.

TURNING PASSION INTO PURPOSEFUL ACTION

Passion isn't something you simply discover—it's something you build through action, experimentation, and resilience. As you try new things, embrace imperfection, and commit to continual learning, you'll find that passion begins to take root and grow. The path won't always be clear, but every step you take brings greater clarity and momentum.

By staying open, acting despite fear, and fueling your journey with curiosity, you position yourself not only to find your passion but to live it fully and impactfully.

REVIEW QUESTIONS

1. Why is it important to start before you feel "ready"?

2. In what ways can embracing imperfection help you move past fear and self-doubt?

3. What fears or doubts have held you back, and how might you begin moving forward despite them?

4. Why is taking action more important than waiting for clarity when it comes to discovering your passion?

5. How can experimenting with small steps lead to clarity about what truly excites you?

6. How does continuous learning help strengthen and sustain passion over time?

7. What role do mentors or supportive people play in helping you pursue your passion?

8. What does "keeping the fire burning" mean to you at this stage of your personal or professional life?

9. What is one small step you can take this week to move closer to living out your passion?

CHAPTER 11

TURNING BELIEF INTO CONSISTENT ACTION

It's not what we do once in a while that shapes
our lives. It's what we do consistently.
—TONY ROBBINS

You've set your goals, visualized the future, and perhaps even begun strong. You know exactly what you want. However, life interferes at some point. You lose motivation, encounter unforeseen setbacks, or become overwhelmed by the sheer effort required to keep going. Does this sound familiar?

The truth is that huge aspirations fail not because they are unachievable but because we fail to act consistently. We tell ourselves we'll start when things "calm down," but life is constantly busy. People who achieve amazing results aren't the most skilled or fortunate—they're the ones who show up every day, regardless of the circumstances.

Now imagine this: You've made up your mind to start running. You buy the gear, create a solid plan, and picture yourself going faster, farther, stronger. For the first few weeks, you're all in—up early, staying disciplined, even eating cleaner. Then one morning, you wake up tired. You skip the run. *Just one day*, you tell yourself. But one day becomes two. Then three. Before you realize it, you've stopped altogether.

The problem wasn't your intention. It wasn't your goal. The issue was that you were depending on motivation to sustain your momentum. But motivation is temporary. It shows up when conditions are perfect—but disappears the moment life gets hard.

Belief, on the other hand, is what keeps you moving when motivation runs out. You need to believe that your consistent actions matter—even when you don't see results right away. It's this kind of belief that bridges the gap between intention and transformation.

Consistency—performing the same acts on a regular and reliable basis—is the secret sauce that turns ambitions into accomplishments. Even when motivation is low, the regular rhythm of daily acts pulls us ahead. It's about developing and sticking to routines to ensure that our behaviors consistently align with our goals. This steadiness fosters trust, both in ourselves and with others, by demonstrating commitment and dependability.

In this chapter, we'll explore how to build a foundation of belief that fuels consistency. You'll learn how to take action even when it feels like nothing is changing and how to stay the course long enough to see your efforts compound. Success isn't built on bursts of effort; it's built on quiet, steady faith in the process. If you've ever started strong but struggled to follow through, this chapter is your turning point.

Let's discover how to keep going—not because it always feels good but because you believe that your small, daily actions are leading somewhere powerful.

SCIENCE BEHIND CONSISTENT ACTION

Our brains are wired to favor routine, and there's a fascinating reason why. In ancient times, routine was essential for survival. Our ancestors didn't have the luxury of unpredictability. They needed to know which routes were safe from predators, where food sources were reliable, and what behaviors would keep them alive. Doing the same thing repeatedly, in the same way, meant safety. Over generations, the brain adapted to prefer familiarity because it conserved energy and reduced risk. That instinct still lives within us today. When we follow routines, our brain doesn't have to work as hard. It switches into a more efficient, automatic mode. When we repeat a task often enough, our brain forms neural pathways that make the behavior easier over time.[1]

This process is called *habituation*. The more we walk the same mental path, the more effortless it becomes. That's why habits—whether helpful or harmful—have such power over us. They require less willpower because they don't feel like decisions anymore; they become second nature.

HARNESSING THE "HABIT LOOP"

How can we harness our brain's desire for consistency? By using something I call the "habit loop." The loop starts with a cue, which triggers the routine, followed by a reward. For example, if you always light a specific candle before sitting down to write, the scent becomes a signal. Your brain begins to associate that smell with focus. If the writing session feels rewarding—maybe you feel productive, proud, or calm—your brain remembers. The next time you light the candle, your brain is already preparing to enter that state.

This same process applies in business. When you commit to showing up daily—whether it's responding to clients, refining your product, or pitching your work—you're strengthening that habit loop. At first, it might feel awkward or exhausting. You may have to force yourself to act, like dragging yourself to the gym on a cold morning. But eventually, those actions become part of your rhythm. The resistance fades, and the behavior becomes part of who you are.

To make this work, you must make your everyday tasks nonnegotiable. That means treating your priorities like promises: not *"I'll try to work on it today"* but *"This is what I'll do, no matter how I feel."* One powerful way to shift your mindset is to anchor your actions to your identity. You don't answer emails because you feel like it; you do it because you're a professional. You don't study your craft only when it's convenient; you do it because you're committed to growth.

Of course, we all face moments of low motivation. You might glance at your calendar and think, *I'm not in the mood.* This is where the brain's love for routine becomes your ally. You can design simple cues to signal that it's time to get into gear, such as playing a specific playlist, brewing a mug of your favorite tea, or sitting in a certain chair that you only use for work. These rituals, though small, help train your brain to shift into action mode.

And don't underestimate the power of reward. Your brain wants to know the effort is worth it. That reward doesn't have to be extravagant. It could be a few minutes of quiet, a walk outside, or simply checking off a box on your progress chart. That sense of closure, of accomplishment, reinforces the habit loop and makes it easier to repeat.

Keep showing up, even when it's hard. The magic isn't in the giant leaps. It's in the steady steps. Consistency turns belief into momentum. And that momentum becomes the force that carries you forward when motivation runs dry.

DEVELOP THE MINDSET FOR CONSISTENT ACTION

Building the right mindset for consistent action isn't about waiting for the perfect conditions—it's about making progress, no matter how small, every single day.

What distinguishes those who succeed from those who struggle is not talent, luck, or even motivation; it is the ability to act on a daily basis, regardless of the circumstances. While motivation can ignite an idea or provide small spurts of energy, it is not dependable.

Discipline, on the other hand, is the constant drive that keeps you moving forward even when your motivation runs low. To start a business or achieve any important objective, you must train your mind to take action consistently, not only when it is convenient. Here's how to cultivate the mindset that will make consistency a habit rather than a struggle.

Shift your focus from motivation to discipline, embrace progress over perfection, and train yourself to take action even when it's hard. Success isn't about grand gestures; it's about the daily commitment to keep going. Keep showing up, and the results will follow.

Shifting from Motivation to Discipline-Driven Action

Relying on motivation is like waiting for the perfect weather to start a journey. Some days may be bright and energizing, while others will be stormy, making progress seem unattainable. This is when discipline comes into play. Discipline is the ability to act despite the circumstances. It's developed through repetition—doing the difficult things repeatedly until they become second nature. Instead of thinking, *Do I feel like doing this today?* change your thinking to *What needs to be done today, regardless of how I feel?*

Consider Serena Williams, for example. She did not become one of the best athletes in history by simply exercising when she felt motivated. She practiced relentlessly, pushing through tiredness and setbacks because she realized that consistency, not occasional effort, leads to excellence. Her routine was famously rigorous: early morning strength training followed by several hours of intense court practice, often six days a week. Even after reaching the top of her game, she maintained a strict schedule that included diet discipline, strategic recovery, and mental training. It wasn't glamorous or always enjoyable, but it was the structure that built her greatness.

Overcoming the "All-or-Nothing" Mindset

Many people sabotage their own success because they believe that if they can't give their best, they shouldn't even attempt. This all-or-nothing mindset keeps entrepreneurs stagnant, waiting for the "perfect" opportunity to begin. However, progress is inherently messy. It's about showing up imperfectly and getting better along the way.

Assume you set a goal of working out five days a week, but you only manage three. Do you decide to quit? No! You appreciate your progress and keep going. The same is true in business: Some days you'll make tremendous strides, while others you'll take small steps. But as long as you're making progress, you're winning. Consistency does not imply perfection; rather, it means refusing to quit.

Taking Action Even When You Don't Feel Like It

One of the most common misconceptions about success is that you must be motivated to do something. In reality, actions generate momentum. The more you show up and take action—even if you don't want to—the simpler it gets.

Think of Walt Disney. Before establishing his empire, he experienced numerous failures. His first animation studio went bankrupt, and he was told he lacked creativity. He even lost the rights to his first successful character, Oswald the Lucky Rabbit, forcing him to start again. Most people would have quit, but Disney relied on self-discipline and unwavering determination. He kept trying, knowing that perseverance would eventually pay off.[2]

Self-discipline is like a muscle: The more you use it, the stronger it becomes. The secret is to start small. If you don't feel like working on your business today, set aside only ten minutes. If you don't want to make the sales call, do it nonetheless. Action is always preferable to inaction.

Rewiring Your Brain for Consistency

Your brain is always adapting to the habits you reinforce. Giving in to procrastination strengthens the habit of avoiding work. However, if you overcome resistance, you train your brain to take action even when it is difficult.

One method is to plan your implementation intentions, which involves selecting when and where you will act—something that aligns well with the SMART habit creation approach discussed in Chapter 6. Instead of telling yourself, *I'll work on my business when I get time*, say, *I'll work on client outreach every day at 10 a.m.* When your actions become predictable, they are considered automatic.

Creating a Nonnegotiable Routine

Think about your most basic routines—brushing your teeth, getting dressed, and eating meals. You don't have to think about them; you just do them. Treating your business or ambitions in the same way avoids the mental struggle of deciding whether to take action. Create a nonnegotiable schedule, whether it's thirty minutes every day to work on your craft or dedicating specific time blocks for business tasks. Sticking to something becomes second nature when it becomes a part of your identity.

Take Emily Weiss, founder of Glossier. Before launching her multimillion-dollar beauty brand, she ran a beauty blog called *Into the Gloss*—while working a full-time job. Her success didn't happen overnight. She committed to waking up at 4:30 a.m. to write blog posts and conduct interviews before heading into the office.[3] This consistent routine not only helped grow her audience but also laid the foundation for what would become Glossier. Weiss didn't wait for perfect conditions—she carved out time, showed up daily, and stuck to her process.

If you schedule your most important duties on a regular basis, they will become automatic. The key is to eliminate the decision-making process. Success is not about willpower; rather, it is about creating systems that automate actions.

Managing Energy, Not Just Time

Many people fail at consistency because they focus only on *time management* when *energy management* is just as important. Pay attention to when you have the most energy and schedule high-priority tasks during those hours. If you're most productive in the morning, tackle critical work then. If you hit an afternoon slump, use that time for less demanding tasks, like responding to emails. Aligning your work with your natural rhythms makes it easier to stay consistent without burning out.

Take Maya Angelou, for example. When writing, she followed a strict routine—working in a rented hotel room from early morning until early afternoon when her mind was sharpest.[4] She didn't push herself to write all day but instead focused on deep, high-quality work during her peak energy hours, allowing her creativity to flow naturally.

The key isn't just to work harder; it's to work smarter. When you align your tasks with your natural energy levels, consistency becomes sustainable, and burnout becomes far less likely. Pay attention to when you feel most focused, and schedule your most demanding tasks during those hours, whether it's strategizing, creating content, or making important decisions. During lower-energy periods, shift to lighter tasks like responding to emails or organizing your workspace, allowing yourself to stay productive without draining your mental resources.

Keeping Yourself Accountable

It's easy to let yourself off the hook when no one is watching. That's why having an accountability system—whether it's a mentor, a mastermind group, or even a simple check-in with a friend—can make a huge difference. When someone else is expecting progress updates from you, you're far more likely to stay committed. Public commitments work too. Announcing your goals on social media or within a community adds an extra layer of accountability that keeps you on track.

CREATE SYSTEMS FOR CONSISTENCY

Consistency is about building systems that make taking action natural and automatic. When you create structured routines and practical processes, you remove guesswork and reduce the effort needed to keep moving forward. Here are a few ways to integrate consistent action into your work:

- **Start with daily personal habits.** For example, commit to spending the first thirty minutes of your workday reviewing your top priorities and setting one clear, achievable goal— whether it's reaching out to three potential clients, refining your marketing plan, or working on product development. This simple habit builds momentum because it gives your day a clear direction every morning.

- **For teams, create and hold regular rituals.** Daily stand-up meetings or brief check-ins aren't just about reporting—they're about creating accountability and focus. These moments encourage steady progress and make it easier to identify challenges early, so you don't lose time or energy.

- **Take advantage of automated tools.** Use tools like scheduling apps to automatically post your social media content, CRM software to follow up on leads without delay, and finance apps that track expenses and cash flow in real time. Automating these repetitive but necessary tasks means you maintain forward momentum even on your busiest or most overwhelming days.

When you combine personal habits, team routines, and smart automation, you build a system where consistency becomes effortless. Instead of battling your willpower, you simply follow the process. Over time, these small, repeated actions add up, creating progress that feels natural and unstoppable.

REALITY OF UNSEEN PROGRESS

Consider planting a seed. You water it every day, but nothing seems to happen for several weeks. It would be easy to conclude that nothing is working and stop watering. But beneath the surface, the seed is doing exactly what it should—growing roots, absorbing nutrients, and preparing to break through the earth. Then one day, a tiny sprout emerges. Even though you couldn't see it, the growth was already underway.

Business operates in the same way. You may be putting in hours of effort—marketing your brand, networking, and refining your products or services—with no visible returns. It's frustrating. It is discouraging. However, just because you can't see the improvement it doesn't mean it's not happening. We need to trust that if we're acting consistently, we're making progress.

Three Phases of Unseen Progress

If you've ever launched a business, you understand the agony of working long hours without seeing instant returns. It's like planting a seed and peering at the earth, wondering when—or if—it will blossom. The truth is that progress occurs in stages, frequently below the surface, before becoming obvious. Understanding these phases will help you overcome skepticism and make sense of your entrepreneurial path.

I like to think of business growth in three stages:

The Invisible Work Phase (1–6 months): This is when most entrepreneurs quit. And it's easy to see why. You are working tirelessly—networking, developing your company strategy, studying the market, and most likely analyzing every decision—but it appears like nothing is happening. Sales may be slow, website traffic is barely a trickle, and your email contains more rejections than prospects.

During this phase, the idea is to focus on the foundation—building brand awareness, establishing industry partnerships, and constantly improving your strategy. Your current efforts may not provide instant results, but they will lay the groundwork for future progress.

Consider this phase to be the equivalent of laying the foundation for a house. Nobody admires the foundation because it is underground and hidden. However, if you do not take the time to construct it strong, the entire structure will eventually collapse.

When the founder of Chobani, Hamdi Ulukaya, purchased an abandoned yogurt factory in 2005, most people thought he had made a mistake. Greek yogurt was not popular in the United States, and he lacked substantial investor support. For the first two years, Ulukaya worked tirelessly behind the scenes, perfecting recipes, testing packaging, and convincing tiny merchants to offer his product. Sales were nearly nonexistent, and development seemed painfully slow.[5]

But he trusted the procedure. Rather than rushing to market without a good product, he concentrated on improving the yogurt and cultivating connections with suppliers. Then, in 2007, he officially launched Chobani. Within a few years, it was one of the best-selling yogurt brands in America.

The Momentum Phase (6–12 months): If you make it through the first six months, congratulations! This is where you begin to witness modest victories—signs that your efforts are paying off. Perhaps a few clients have finally signed on, or a collaboration possibility arises. You begin receiving inquiries rather than always chasing leads. But progress feels slow, and success is far from certain.

The biggest mistake entrepreneurs make during this stage is slowing down when they notice minor progress. Instead, focus on what's working—increase marketing efforts, build your network, and continue to improve your product or service. The goal is to build on those early successes and achieve long-term growth.

Momentum in business is similar to moving a large boulder up a hill: Initially, it goes quite slowly, but with constant effort, it begins to change, making it simpler to push.

Consider Calendly, founded by Tope Awotona. In the beginning, Awotona poured his life savings into developing the tool after becoming frustrated with the endless back-and-forth of scheduling meetings. He faced numerous setbacks, including a failed initial development team, but he pressed on—bootstrapping the company while refining the product based on user feedback. Growth was slow at first, but he focused on delivering a simple, clean solution to a real problem. Early adopters spread the word, and eventually, small wins snowballed into widespread adoption. Today, Calendly is used by millions, proving that momentum can turn quiet beginnings into global impact.[6]

The Breakthrough Phase (12+ months): This is the phase that every entrepreneur dreams of: when their hard work finally pays off. At this point, unexpected opportunities arise. Your brand is recognized, consumers trust your company, and revenue becomes more predictable. It doesn't mean that obstacles go away; rather, you now have systems, customers, and credibility working in your favor.

During this stage, growth appears exponential. However, this only happens if you've been consistent during the first two phases. This is when you can begin scaling, delegating, and extending your firm in previously unimaginable ways.

While some entrepreneurs experience breakthroughs around the one-year mark, it's important to understand that timelines aren't set in stone. If your journey is moving more slowly, that doesn't mean you're failing—it means you're building deliberately. Some businesses take longer to find their rhythm, especially when experimenting with different strategies or navigating unpredictable markets. Stay consistent. Often, slow and steady progress builds the strongest, most sustainable success stories.

Take Tory Burch, for example. In 2004, she launched her fashion label from her kitchen table with a small boutique in Manhattan and a vision to offer affordable luxury. The early days were far from glamorous. She handled everything, from design to logistics, and poured herself into building a brand with both substance and style. Her big break came not in year one but after Oprah Winfrey featured her on her show a year later.[7] That exposure catapulted her into the spotlight, but it was Burch's preparation, consistency, and the systems she had already put in place that allowed her to seize the moment and scale.

Today, Tory Burch is a globally recognized fashion brand with hundreds of stores worldwide. Her success wasn't just the result of one lucky moment—it was the outcome of steady action, clear vision, and systems that could support growth when opportunity knocked.

ALIGN YOUR ACTIONS WITH YOUR FUTURE SELF

One of the most powerful shifts I made was asking myself, *If I already had what I wanted, how would I act?* The version of me who had built a multimillion-dollar company, who led boldly in a male-dominated industry—how would she carry herself?

So, I started speaking with authority about the vision I had, even when I was the only one who believed in it. I talked about future projects as though they were already in motion. I walked into rooms with my shoulders back and my head high, introducing myself with certainty and clarity, even when I felt shaky inside. I reached out to business mentors I thought were far beyond my reach, pitched bold ideas in meetings where I once would've stayed silent, and held my ground when I knew my ideas were right, even when others disagreed. I stopped asking for permission and started claiming my space.

These were the courageous things I did.

And I grew out of my childhood—not in age, but in mindset. I let go of the need to please everyone. I stopped shrinking myself to make others comfortable. I stopped doubting that I belonged in the room. As a child, I learned to wait for approval, to avoid conflict, to play small. But stepping into my future self meant leaving those patterns behind. I had to start making decisions not from fear or habit but from vision and leadership.

What I mean here is "future self-alignment." I stopped basing my choices on where I was and began acting as the woman I was becoming. If I wanted to be a bold, strategic, visionary CEO, I had to lead that way now—not later.

You cannot achieve success by waiting until you feel like the person you want to be. You must act like that person today—and trust that your beliefs, confidence, and results will catch up.

TRUSTING THE PROCESS EVEN WHEN IMMEDIATE RESULTS AREN'T VISIBLE

In Chapter 9, we looked at how evidence and reinforcement help form beliefs. However, belief without action remains stagnant. Acting on faith entails moving forward before evidence appears.

Today's modern Western culture is preoccupied with instant gratification, especially in entrepreneurial circles. We expect rapid results from our efforts, and when they don't happen as swiftly as we had planned, skepticism sets in. You create a company page, engage in branding, and frequently share valuable material. You expect interaction and sales to increase, but after a month, the response is low. The temptation to give up is strong—after all, if people don't respond now, will they ever?

What you don't notice are the quiet observers: potential clients who are watching before deciding to interact. The breakthrough occurs months later, when one major client contacts you because they've been watching your work all along.

This pattern of delayed response is not unique. It shows up in different areas of your business, often when you least expect it. Just when you think your efforts are going unnoticed, something begins to shift beneath the surface—slowly, quietly, but with real momentum.

You invest in a new product for your company, promote it diligently, and send emails to potential customers. You expected a flood of interest, but sales came in slowly. Doubt comes in, and you question if you made the incorrect decision. Then, apparently out of nowhere, a huge opportunity arises—a bulk order from a firm, a blog feature, or an influencer promoting your product—proving that all your hard work was not in vain.

As entrepreneurs, particularly as women starting enterprises in areas that are frequently dominated by men, impatience may be our worst enemy. But here's the truth: Success is rarely immediate. Financial stability, brand recognition, and devoted customers are all results that require time to achieve.

KEEP SHOWING UP

At the end of the day, success isn't about bursts of motivation or waiting for the perfect moment—it's about showing up, day in and day out. It's about rewiring your brain to prioritize action over hesitation, treating your goals like nonnegotiable commitments, managing your energy wisely, and holding yourself accountable.

The truth is, consistency isn't glamorous. It's not always exciting, and it won't always feel rewarding in the moment. But over time, the small, repeated actions compound into extraordinary results. The best-selling book, the thriving business, the strong and healthy body—they all come from doing the work even when you don't feel like it.

So, as you move forward, ask yourself: *Who do I want to become? A person who waits for motivation, or someone who takes action regardless of how they feel?* The choice is yours. And the best part? You don't have to get it perfect. You just have to get started. Keep showing up, and success will take care of itself.

REVIEW QUESTIONS

1. How does reinforcing certain habits shape the way your brain functions?

2. Why is it important to create a nonnegotiable routine when working toward a goal?

3. What is an implementation intention, and how can it help with consistency?

4. What's the difference between managing time and managing energy?

5. Why is it important to align tasks with your natural energy levels?

6. What role does accountability play in maintaining consistency?

7. How can public commitments help reinforce discipline?

8. What role does creating a system or routine play in building lasting consistency?

CHAPTER 12

ACTING TO OVERCOME OBSTACLES

You may encounter many defeats,
but you must not be defeated.
—MAYA ANGELOU

Every entrepreneur dreams of success—the thriving business, the financial freedom, the ability to create something meaningful. In the United States alone, hundreds of thousands of new businesses are launched every month. In 2023, a staggering 5.5 million new business applications were filed.[1] The allure is clear—being your own boss, pursuing a passion, and building something from the ground up. But what often gets left out of the conversation are the roadblocks along the way. No matter how solid your business plan is, obstacles will come—unexpected cash flow shortages, clients defaulting on payments, economic downturns, low sales, or even self-doubt creeping in at the worst possible moment.

I remember a time when my business was teetering on the edge. It was early 2023, and we had just expanded our lending services, confident that we had built a strong client base. But within months, things started unraveling. Several high-value clients—who together owed nearly $500,000—started delaying payments, and some completely defaulted. Meanwhile, overhead costs were piling up. Payroll, rent, marketing expenses all had to be paid, whether the clients honored their commitments or not. I had a team of five employees relying on me, and at one point, our business account was down. The weight of responsibility was crushing.

I remember sitting in my office late at night, staring at the numbers from my accountant, trying to figure out a way forward. Was this just a temporary setback, or was it the beginning of the end? Many entrepreneurs find themselves in this exact moment—when self-doubt meets financial pressure, and every decision feels like walking a tightrope over disaster. If you've ever had to delay paying yourself just to keep the lights on, if you've ever questioned whether your business will survive another month, then you know this feeling.

But how do you recognize when you're facing a normal challenge versus when you're at a true breaking point? The signs are clear: Your revenue can't cover your expenses, your stress is making you second-guess every decision, and the excitement that once fueled you is now replaced by survival mode. If you find yourself in this situation, you're not alone.

In this chapter, we'll explore the common obstacles entrepreneurs face across all industries—not just lending but business ownership as a whole. We'll break down the financial, emotional, and strategic challenges that threaten to derail businesses and, more importantly, the proven ways to push through them. Because success isn't about avoiding obstacles—it's about learning how to overcome them.

IDENTIFYING WHAT HOLDS US BACK

In Chapter 7, we looked at what might hold us back from believing in ourselves and the success of our business. Now, let's dig a little deeper so you can act to overcome the obstacles that might hold you back beyond just your beliefs.

The entrepreneurial path is frequently glamorized, with stories of grit, determination, and ultimate success dominating the news. However, behind every success story lie instances of difficulty, reluctance, and dissatisfaction. Many entrepreneurs' hardest struggles are internal rather than external. Overcoming these unseen barriers is just as important as dealing with market fluctuations or financial disappointments.

IDENTIFYING INTERNAL OBSTACLES

Before you can overcome external challenges, you must first recognize the internal ones that quietly hold you back. These hidden barriers often shape your decisions and dampen your momentum without you even realizing it.

Self-Doubt

Self-doubt does not discriminate. It seeps in whether you're just getting started or have been doing it for years. Even the most successful entrepreneurs face self-doubt. It sneaks in during difficult times—when a significant transaction fails, when competition becomes insurmountable, or when business growth slows.

Self-doubt causes people to second-guess their decisions, hesitate on opportunities, and, in some cases, sabotage their own success, owing to a lack of belief in their own abilities. The key is to recognize that self-doubt is natural, and it only has power over you if you allow it. Rather than avoiding feelings of self-doubt, acknowledge them. Ask yourself if your fear is founded on facts or preconceptions. Self-doubt is typically an emotional response rather than a logical response.

The best method to overcome self-doubt is to take action. Small accomplishments, mentorship, and a strong support system can boost confidence and remind you why you started in the first place.

Payal Kadakia, the founder of ClassPass, serves as an excellent example. Before ClassPass established a game-changing fitness subscription service, Kadakia grappled with self-doubt. She quit a comfortable corporate career at Bain & Company to venture into entrepreneurship, but her first start-up idea did not work. She was constantly questioning whether she was making the correct decisions, especially after receiving multiple investor rejections and doubts about her idea.[2]

Instead of allowing skepticism to paralyze her, she improved her approach. She shifted her focus to solving a problem she was passionate about: making it easy for people to find and book fitness programs. This resulted in the founding of ClassPass, which has grown into a global brand with millions of users.

Decision Paralysis

As an entrepreneur, you are always making decisions—hiring the right people, developing marketing strategies, managing funds, and planning for expansion. The sheer number of options can be daunting, and before you realize it, you're caught in a loop of overthinking. You might analyze every conceivable conclusion, hoping for the perfect answer, but perfection does not exist.

To overcome decision paralysis, trust yourself. Collect the essential facts, assess the risks, and make a choice. No decision is ever perfect, but action propels you forward, whereas hesitation keeps you stuck. Even if you make the wrong decision, you'll learn from it and be prepared to pivot if necessary. The worst option is to make no decision at all.

Reid Hoffman, cofounder of LinkedIn, is an excellent example of how to break free from decision paralysis. Before launching LinkedIn, Hoffman had to decide whether to leave behind the security of his role at PayPal to build a new kind of professional network—something that many believed wouldn't work. He could have easily kept debating whether the market was ready or waited for the perfect time. Instead, he gathered input, accepted the risks, and took decisive action. His willingness to move forward despite uncertainty laid the foundation for what became the world's largest professional networking platform.[3]

Founder's Guilt

Building a business requires all of your time, energy, and attention. But have you ever felt guilty about ignoring your family, missing key events, or simply not being there as you should be? That internal tension can drain you, causing burnout and even self-sabotage.

Set clear limits rather than allowing guilt to overtake you. When it comes to relationships, prioritize quality above quantity. When you're with family or loved ones, be fully present. Put your phone away, switch off from "work mode," and truly engage. Scheduling time for family and friends, just like you would for an important business meeting, allows you to strike a healthier balance while maintaining your success.

Katrina Lake, the creator of Stitch Fix, grappled with the enormous burden of operating a business while raising a family as she grew Stitch Fix into a successful, publicly traded corporation. In 2017, she became the youngest woman to take a company public while pregnant, yet she frequently felt guilty for not being present enough at home. Balancing high-stakes leadership with parenthood was difficult, and she had to make difficult choices about where to direct her time and energy.[4]

Lake learned to value quality above quantity in her personal life in order to be completely engaged with her family. She also tried to create a workplace culture that values work-life balance, setting a good example for other working parents. Her story demonstrates how success and family life may coexist when conscious boundaries and priorities are established.

Resistance to Delegation

If you've ever convinced yourself, *It's just easier if I do it myself*, you are not alone. Many entrepreneurs struggle to delegate because they believe no one else can complete tasks as well as they can. However, attempting to do everything alone is not a sign of dedication; rather, it is a quick pathway to burnout.

The truth is that you cannot scale a business unless you trust others. Delegation is more than simply handing over responsibilities; it is about forming a strong team and empowering them to manage tasks effectively. Begin small by outsourcing regular tasks, assigning projects to qualified staff, and giving them the freedom to own their jobs. When you quit micromanaging and instead focus on big-picture strategy, you'll see your business expand in ways you never could have imagined.

Sophia Amoruso, the founder of Nasty Gal and Girlboss, grappled with letting go of control as she transformed Nasty Gal from a little eBay company to a multimillion-dollar fashion empire. She was deeply involved in every part of the business, from customer service to creative direction, and she believed that no one could better execute her vision than she could. This unwillingness to delegate resulted in overwork, decision fatigue, and, eventually, difficulties in scaling the organization efficiently.[5]

As Nasty Gal grew, she recognized the importance of developing a strong leadership team and delegating essential responsibilities to others. She was able to focus on strategic expansion rather than day-to-day operations after learning how to successfully delegate.

This demonstrates that trusting your team and letting go of micromanagement are critical for long-term success.

Perfectionism

If you've ever put off launching a product, running a marketing campaign, or expanding your business because it wasn't "perfect" yet, you may be suffering from perfectionism. Striving for perfection is admirable, but stressing over every minor detail can hinder your progress and leave you trapped in an endless loop of modifications.

What is the truth? Perfection is just an illusion. The most successful entrepreneurs take action, put their work out there, and keep improving as they go. Instead of waiting for the perfect version, release the best version you can right now and refine it based on customer feedback. Progress always triumphs over perfection—because a firm that never moves forward will never flourish.

Miki Agrawal, the cofounder of Thinx and TUSHY, struggled with perfectionism when she first launched her innovative period-proof underwear brand, Thinx. She wanted the product, branding, and messaging to be impeccable before launching. However, she understood that waiting for things to be "perfect" was preventing her from progressing. Instead, she released the best possible version and adapted it based on client feedback.[6]

This mindset shift enabled Thinx to disrupt the feminine hygiene sector, and Agrawal later used the same strategy with TUSHY, her bidet start-up. Agrawal created many successful businesses that broke industry norms and transformed customer behaviors by focusing on execution rather than continuous refinement.

Fatigue

Running a firm entails constantly reacting to new technologies, market developments, and unanticipated interruptions. While adaptation is critical for survival in business, the constant urge to pivot can wear you down. If you feel like you're constantly reacting rather than moving forward, you may be suffering from adaptation fatigue.

How do you overcome this? Stop following every fad and instead focus on your basic values and long-term goals. Yes, modifications are important, but not every shift necessitates a total rebuild. When you base your decisions on fundamental business principles, you may generate stability in unpredictable times. Instead of feeling overwhelmed, you will approach change with confidence and purpose.

Stick to your foundation, pace yourself, and let your values guide your growth. That's how you outlast fatigue and thrive.

CONFRONTING EXTERNAL OBSTACLES

While internal struggles need new ways of thinking, external problems need strategic solutions. Entrepreneurs must learn to deal with problems that are often out of their control, like doubts about their business or financial hurdles.

Managing Cash Flow Challenges and Financial Setbacks

Cash flow is the lifeblood of your business. When it gets messed up, it feels like everything is at risk. Clients who don't pay on time, rising operational costs, and sudden downturns in the economy can really put a strain on your funds. You are not the only one who has to deal with these problems—every business owner does. Not only is escaping them important, but so is preparing for them before they happen.

TIPS TO AVOID FINANCIAL PITFALLS

Finances are the heart of any business. Here are some practical steps to stay out of the red:

- **Secure your billing system:** Make sure there are clear payment terms in your contracts. Use invoicing software that allows you to set up automatic reminders. Don't hesitate to charge late fees when necessary. Prompt payments help keep your operations running smoothly.

- **Build a financial safety net:** An emergency fund, even one that covers just two to three months of expenses, can offer breathing room when cash flow slows down. It gives you time to make thoughtful decisions instead of acting out of desperation.

- **Diversify your income streams:** Relying on one source of income is risky. Create multiple revenue streams to build financial stability. Here are some examples of other revenue streams:

  - Launch a new product line or service.

  - Offer paid workshops or consulting based on your expertise.

  - Create digital products such as ebooks or online courses.

  - Develop a subscription-based offering for recurring income.

  - Explore affiliate partnerships or passive income opportunities.

- **Don't wait until you're desperate to build financial relationships:** Build some links with lenders as soon as possible, look into business lines of credit, and look into grants or other ways to get money. When it comes to money, having more options will help you get through tough times. Remember that problems with money will always be there, but they don't have to be crippling if you know what to do.

Navigating Market Fluctuations

Economic downturns, industry changes, and severe competition can shake even the strongest companies. One moment, demand is high; the next, market conditions change. It's natural to be unsure whether to pivot or stay the course, but waiting for too long might jeopardize your business.

The key is to remain ahead of the curve. Keep an eye on market trends—read industry reports, study emerging technology, and monitor changes in customer behavior. Most importantly, listen to your customers. Their needs and preferences are continuously changing, and organizations that adapt to these changes remain competitive while others fade away.

Handling Competitive Pressure

When faced with fierce competition, don't panic; instead, differentiate. What makes your business stand out? Perhaps it's your customer service, distinctive product options, or innovative approach. Lean into your strengths and refine them even more. At the same time, don't hesitate to adjust your business plan as needed. The most successful businesses are not simply those with the strongest ideas but those that are willing to grow while remaining true to their objective.

Managing Client Expectations

Your clients are the lifeblood of your business, but let's be honest: Not all of them are easy to manage. Some anticipate immediate results, while others try to negotiate lower prices, and a few may be slow when it comes to payment for products or services. If you do not establish boundaries early, you will find yourself continuously pressured, overworked, and devalued.

How do you overcome this? Clear and up-front communication is essential. Be open and honest about cost, timing, and what is really possible from the beginning. Spell out deliverables in writing—contracts, agreements, or thorough proposals can help minimize future misunderstandings. If a client demands anything unreasonable, don't be scared to stay firm. Position yourself as an expert, not simply a service provider.

Building Trust

Consistency, rather than just words, is what builds trust. Keep your promises, be professional even in difficult situations, and resolve problems diplomatically. Businesses that prosper do not say yes to everything; rather, they set expectations, produce quality, and foster mutually respectful relationships.

Trust also grows when you communicate openly and take responsibility for mistakes. Be transparent about setbacks or delays instead of hiding them. Listen actively to feedback from clients and team members, and show that you value their input by acting on it. Small actions such as responding to messages promptly, following up on commitments, and treating every interaction with care reinforce that you are dependable and trustworthy. Over time, this reliability becomes your reputation, attracting loyal customers, committed employees, and supportive partners.

Staying Connected to Sales

In the early days of a start-up, founders frequently wear numerous hats, including that of salesperson. After all, who knows the product or service better than the one who created it? However, when the company expands and the team increases, many entrepreneurs begin to delegate the sales process. They transfer their focus to finance, operations, and management, expecting that their sales team will handle everything. This is where things may go wrong.

For example, Jessica Alba, founder of The Honest Company, faced relentless pressure to keep expanding her product line to compete with bigger brands. Investors and retailers wanted faster growth and more products on shelves, but Alba refused to chase every new idea if it meant compromising on the company's commitment to safe, eco-friendly ingredients. When early product issues arose—like when customers complained that their sunscreen was too greasy and left a white residue on their skin—instead of quickly changing formulas to follow cheaper trends, she doubled down on research and quality testing to maintain trust. By resisting constant pivots and focusing on Honest's core mission of transparency and safety, Alba avoided burnout and built a lasting, billion-dollar brand.[7]

While a founder cannot do everything, fully separating from sales can leave you unprepared when issues arise.

You do not need to supervise every transaction, but remaining informed is critical. Keep an eye on performance patterns, listen to consumer feedback, and be prepared to step in if necessary. And most importantly, don't neglect your sales team. They require constant training, support, and a thorough knowledge of your goals. A well-equipped sales team does more than just complete deals; they shape the destiny of your firm.

So, regardless of how busy you are, make sales a priority. It's critical for your business.

Setting Strategic Pricing

Setting the proper price for your products or services can be like walking a tightrope. Many small business owners struggle with pricing, allowing emotions such as fear or pride to take over. Perhaps you are frightened of losing a sale, so you undercharge. Or maybe you're caught up in the thrill of outbidding competitors and securing a contract at any price. But here's the harsh reality: Emotional pricing can harm your bottom line and cause long-term financial stress.

Price with your head, not your heart. Know your costs inside and out, keep an eye on industry developments, and periodically examine how your pricing compares to competitors. A well-thought-out approach ensures that you're profiting rather than merely selling.

What if customers aren't biting? Don't guess. Ask. Many buyers are ready to provide feedback on pricing, and their views might help you improve your approach. The trick is to price with confidence and understand the value you bring to the table. When you accomplish this, your company becomes more sustainable, profitable, and robust.

Breaking Stereotypes and Building Credibility

There is still bias in many fields, and you may have experienced it yourself. When others doubt you because of bias—whether it's about your age, background, or gender—it can make growing your business feel impossible.

In the financial services sector, credibility is everything. Yet according to a 2022 report by Deloitte, women hold only 24 percent of senior leadership roles in global financial services firms, and fewer than 8 percent of CEOs in this space are women.[8] The gap is even more stark for younger women, who often face the compounded challenge of being perceived as inexperienced, emotional, or not authoritative enough in boardrooms and client meetings. Many still see leadership in finance as something that comes with gray hair and a deep voice—not youth and femininity.

One of the biggest external challenges I faced was securing credibility in the lending space. Partners and clients often didn't want to work with a mortgage firm that was owned by a woman. I didn't let this stop me; instead, I honed my skills, gave the best service possible, and built an image that didn't depend on my gender.

How did I do it? First, I became concerned with being the best at my job. I kept up with market trends, learned all about the rules that apply to my business, and established myself as a thought leader by sharing my ideas through webinars and networking events. When people heard my name, they associated it with deep industry knowledge and reliability.

Next, I made sure that my service was so exceptional that customers couldn't ignore the value I brought. I streamlined processes to speed up and improve the efficiency of mortgage approvals. I also made sure that every contact with a client was unique and no detail was missed. I not only met the standards of my field but also went above and beyond them.

You can do the same thing in your field. Become the go-to expert by always learning more, participating in discussions about your field, and making a strong name for yourself in your market. Focus on providing exceptional service that makes you stand out, whether it's through new ideas, great customer service, or close attention to detail. Bias doesn't matter when your work speaks for itself.

HOW TO CONTINUE MOVING FORWARD, EVEN WHEN RESULTS ARE SLOW

Building a business or pursuing any worthwhile objective involves highs and lows. The enthusiasm of starting strong is frequently met with the reality of gradual growth, which can lead to self-doubt. Slow progress can be irritating, but it does not indicate failure. Growth frequently occurs behind the scenes before the effects are obvious. Instead of allowing doubt to take control, focus on strategic tasks that will keep you going forward. Every setback is an opportunity to refine your approach and reinforce your foundation.

Here are some practical strategies for maintaining pace and moving through slow seasons with confidence. This section specifically explores areas such as marketing funnels, realistic expectations, and essential business-building tactics to help you stay focused and intentional.

Detach from Immediate Outcomes

It's easy to become obsessed with numbers—sales figures, website traffic, and social media engagement. However, if you base your drive on rapid outcomes, you will burn out soon in business. As female entrepreneurs, we pour our hearts into our businesses, and when results do not appear quickly, frustration sets in. We begin to wonder if we are doing enough, if we should pivot, or if success is even meant for us.

But here's the truth: Focusing too much on instant results depletes your energy and motivation. Instead, concentrate on what you can control—sharpen your abilities, improve your offerings, and constantly show up for your business. Sharpen your abilities by attending industry workshops, enrolling in online courses, finding a mentor, or setting aside regular time each week to read, study trends, or practice your craft. Improve your offerings might mean surveying your customers for feedback, refining your product or service based on what they need most, testing new features, or even enhancing your branding and packaging. Keep showing up by sticking to a consistent content schedule, staying visible on your platforms, and following through with your commitments—especially when motivation fades.

Growth is not always obvious at first, but that doesn't imply it doesn't occur. Your success is founded on constant action, not overnight victories. Remember: The growth you can't see now is laying the groundwork for the breakthrough you'll have tomorrow. Trust yourself and your effort, and, most importantly, keep going.

In March of 2025, I worked with the owner of a small catering business who was on the verge of shutting down due to a sudden drop in bookings and increasing overhead costs. With outstanding invoices piling up and her kitchen lease nearly unpaid, she felt overwhelmed and unsure if continuing was even worth it.

I encouraged her to shift focus toward what she could control. I told her, "Refine your finances, maintain consistent follow-ups with clients, and believe in the process." She took that to heart. She restructured her menu offerings to cut food waste, renegotiated payment terms with vendors, and reached out to past clients with a special promotion. She also started offering smaller-scale catering options to appeal to budget-conscious customers.

Within three months, she had booked enough events to stabilize her income, regained her footing, and even hired part-time help. Her business didn't just recover—it came back more agile and efficient than before.

Reevaluate Your Strategy Without Overhauling Everything

When growth is slow, the natural tendency is to scrap everything and start again. But before you push the reset button, take a step back and reassess. You don't always need to start from scratch; small, strategic changes can make a big change.

Consider if you were to modify a recipe. If a dish doesn't turn out as desired, you don't discard all the ingredients—you tweak the seasoning, adjust the heat, or change the cooking time. The same applies to your business.

Instead of overhauling your entire approach, pinpoint what's working and what's not. Perhaps your messaging needs to be more compelling, your pricing increased to reflect the value you offer, or your target demographic fine-tuned—maybe your ideal customer isn't women in their early twenties but professional women in their early thirties looking for more tailored solutions.

I once worked with an entrepreneur who ran an online skincare shop. She was discouraged by what she described as "low engagement" on her website—very few clicks on product pages, high bounce rates, and almost no newsletter sign-ups. She expected her social media following to convert into sales, but it wasn't happening. Instead of scrapping her site or changing her product line, she made focused improvements: rewriting her product descriptions to speak directly to customer pain points, adding testimonials, and using more persuasive calls to action. Within five weeks, her conversion rate rose by 15 percent.

Success is achieved through thoughtful, targeted modifications rather than perpetual innovation. Maintain what works, improve what doesn't, and believe that small changes yield great results. Keep going!

Invest in Skills That Will Directly Impact Growth

When results are slow, it's easy to become stuck. Instead of waiting for things to change, take action by honing the skills that will propel your company forward. Growth requires not only hard work but also smart work.

Ask yourself: *What is the one skill that, if mastered, would have the greatest impact?* Perhaps it's increasing your sales skills, understanding digital marketing, or becoming a better negotiator. Concentrate on gaining skills that will immediately affect your bottom line.

As Warren Buffett says, "By far the best investment you can make is yourself." As humans, we are constantly focused on the external world. But one of my favorite mantras, and an excellent reminder, is that everything we ever want in life is already within us. This is why I spend a lot of my time leveling up myself and my mindset. Because when I increase my knowledge and self-study, I can show up that much better for those around me. That's why it's essential to intentionally carve out time to invest in yourself.

You don't need to wait for the perfect moment. Attend a workshop or mastermind that aligns with your goals. Enroll in an online course to sharpen your skills. Even a quiet retreat or focused day of self-study can help you reconnect with your purpose and strategy. When you commit to growing yourself, you naturally show up stronger and more prepared for those around you—and for your business.

Test New Customer Acquisition Channels

When your business's results are slow, it can be tempting to keep pushing harder in the same direction. But what if the actual solution lies in forging a new path? If your existing customer acquisition strategies aren't working, it's time to try a new approach.

This is where understanding the marketing funnel becomes essential. The funnel typically begins with awareness (getting your brand noticed), followed by interest, consideration, and finally conversion (a sale). Many new entrepreneurs focus only on awareness—posting on social media or running ads—without nurturing prospects through the remaining stages. To build momentum, you need strategies for every stage of that funnel.

Think about where your ideal customers hang out. Ask yourself: *Am I relying only on social media while ignoring email marketing, SEO, or community engagement? Am I investing in ads but overlooking strategic partnerships—collaborations with others in my field who serve a similar audience?* These partnerships could look like guest podcast appearances, cohosted events, shout-outs in newsletters, or even product bundles with complementary brands. If you're new to the industry, begin by identifying people whose work aligns with yours. Reach out respectfully, offer value first, and be open to collaboration that benefits both parties. Sometimes, a simple change can make all the difference.

In 2023, I worked with a nutrition coach who was struggling to generate leads through her Instagram page. Despite posting consistently, engagement was low, and inquiries were almost nonexistent. After reassessing her approach, she decided to host three free webinars over a six-week period to showcase her expertise and build trust with her target audience.

To promote the webinars, she took the following steps:

- Shared the event in relevant Facebook groups

- Collaborated with a fitness influencer who mentioned the event in her stories

- Sent a series of emails to her small but growing subscriber list

- Posted countdown reminders on Instagram and LinkedIn

Her goal was to educate, not just sell—so she offered valuable content on topics like meal planning, sugar detox, and sustainable weight loss. By the end of six weeks, fifteen new clients had signed up for her coaching program, many of whom said they wouldn't have discovered her otherwise.

If you're not seeing results, it might be time to try a new approach. Here are a few customer acquisition channels you can explore:

- Free webinars or live workshops—educate and connect with your audience

- Consistent email marketing—nurture leads and stay top of mind

- Social media advertising—use targeted ads to reach specific demographics

- SEO and blogging—drive traffic through helpful, keyword-rich content

- Strategic partnerships—team up with complementary businesses to share audiences

- Podcast interviews or guest speaking—showcase your expertise on other platforms

Experimenting with even one new channel can open doors you never expected. Growth often begins where your comfort zone ends—so stay open, stay creative, and stay committed.

Create a Visibility Plan Rather Than Just Posting Content

Social media can be one of the most powerful—and cost-effective—tools for building your business. But simply posting random content without a plan is like throwing darts in the dark: You might hit something once in a while, but it's mostly guesswork.

Instead of hoping for engagement, create a visibility strategy that intentionally puts your brand in front of the right people—consistently and with purpose.

One entrepreneur I mentored, a self-taught skincare formulator, was discouraged by the poor engagement on her business Instagram account, despite posting daily product photos and promotional captions. Her posts were consistent but not strategic. We reviewed her audience insights and shifted to posting more educational videos, behind-the-scenes content, and customer testimonials. We also collaborated with micro-influencers in the skincare space. Within five months, her reach grew by over 400 percent, and she started seeing regular sales from social media.

Visibility is about showing up with purpose. And that purpose is rooted in your "why." Back in Chapter 2, you reflected deeply on your purpose—your reason for starting this business. Now is the time to bring that "why" front and center in your visibility efforts. Let it guide how you show up online and how you connect with your audience. Your purpose fuels your message, and your message draws the right people in. Show up with your "why," engage with your audience meaningfully, and watch your brand awareness grow.

CREATING YOUR CONTENT STRATEGY

Where do my ideal customers spend their time online? Are they scrolling through Instagram, joining Facebook groups, watching YouTube tutorials, or reading LinkedIn articles? What types of content appeal to them?

To figure this out, you can

- Look at your competitors' most engaged posts.
- Use tools like Answer the Public, Google Trends, or BuzzSumo to explore trending topics and questions in your field.
- Pay attention to what your audience engages with most—reels, stories, carousels, blog posts, etc.

Here's your action plan:

- Choose one to two platforms to focus on.
- Decide on a few core content themes (e.g., education, inspiration, behind the scenes).
- Plan a content calendar—post consistently, not randomly.
- Track performance and tweak your approach.

FOCUS ON WHAT'S IN YOUR CONTROL

As an entrepreneur, there may be times when progress seems frustratingly slow. You may wonder if all your efforts are paying off, especially if others appear to be making faster progress. But here's the truth: Focusing on what you can't change, whether it's market trends, competition, or unanticipated delays, drains your energy and stifles your momentum.

Instead of being frustrated, focus on the one thing you always have control over: your own actions. You have control over your everyday effort, the techniques you employ, and the resilience you bring to the table. Every step you take, however small, is a stride forward. Success is rarely about unexpected breakthroughs; it is about constant work, even if the rewards do not appear right away.

Your perspective has a major impact on how you handle slow progress. If you constantly compare your progress to that of others, you will always feel like you are behind. Remember, success is a personal journey, not a race. Instead of looking at others, concentrate on improving your own game.

Ask yourself: *What can I do today to move the needle forward? How can I hone my skills, improve my services, or develop relationships with my clients?* Maybe it's something as simple as watching a ten-minute tutorial, rewriting your service description for clarity, sending a thank-you message to a loyal customer, or reaching out to someone you've been meaning to connect with. These small, manageable steps build momentum, especially on days when everything feels like too much. When you focus on growth rather than speed, you'll notice that each challenge is transforming you into a stronger, wiser businesswoman.

Furthermore, persistence is essential. Many of the most successful entrepreneurs endured long periods of small progress before making their breakthroughs. The distinction between those who succeed and those who fail is simple: They persevered. They concentrated on showing up every day, learning from setbacks, and improving their strategy.

So, if you feel things aren't moving quickly enough, take a step back and remember why you started. Celebrate the small victories, because they add up. Recognize that even slow growth is progress. Most crucial, stay focused on the things you can control—your effort, attitude, and conviction in yourself. The results will come.

TURN CHALLENGES INTO CATALYSTS FOR GROWTH

You've already addressed internal struggles such as decision paralysis, perfectionism, and founder's guilt. By identifying and eliminating these limits, you have removed any mental hurdles that may have been holding you back.

Now, as you face external obstacles such as cash flow issues, market upheavals, and competition, you need a strategy to keep your firm moving forward. Financial discipline, sound decision-making, and staying current on industry developments will help you weather any storm. By keeping informed, honing your skills, and practicing financial discipline, you can position yourself for growth regardless of the challenges. Every setback presents an opportunity to learn, grow, and build your business.

At the end of the day, it's not about avoiding challenges; it's about learning to pivot, adapt, and persevere. You'll need to continually build resilience and develop your adaptability. Because let's be honest: Entrepreneurship is not simple or easy. Each obstacle you overcome sharpens, strengthens, and prepares you for the next task. Stay focused and adaptive, and keep moving forward—you are more than capable of overcoming any obstacle that comes your way.

Keep going. You've got this.

REVIEW QUESTIONS

1. Why is financial discipline important for entrepreneurs, and what can be done to enhance cash-flow management?

2. What are some proactive strategies for dealing with late payments from clients?

3. What strategies can entrepreneurs use to diversify their revenue streams and reduce financial risks?

4. How do entrepreneurs stay ahead of market shifts and competition pressures?

5. Why is clear and up-front communication important when managing client expectations?

6. What role does customer service play in differentiating a business from its competitors?

7. What typical industry misconceptions may entrepreneurs confront, and how can they overcome them?

8. How did the author gain a reputation in the lending industry despite early skepticism?

9. Why is adaptability essential in business, and how can entrepreneurs cultivate it?

10. How does resilience contribute to long-term business success?

CHAPTER 13

HARNESSING THE POWER OF THE PAUSE

The quieter you become, the more you can hear.
—RAM DASS

Most of my life, I have lived in high-paced environments. When I was eighteen and modeling, it meant going from casting call to casting call in NYC, hoping to be booked for jobs and accepting jobs sometimes at the last minute and moving my schedule around—all while I waitressed at high-end nightclubs so I could afford to pursue my passion for starting my own business as an entrepreneur. I lived most of my life with no set direction and a flexible schedule, which led to a lot of jumping on planes to Miami for last-minute trips with friends and exploring the night scene with the friends I surrounded myself with back then—people who thrived on spontaneity and night-life. I lived with a go-go-go mentality, where I thought hoping on every opportunity was the right thing to do.

Before I knew it, life was happening for me at such a fast pace that it began to take a negative spiral, with close relationships ending, a breakup, and change within my job all happening at the same time. I had no tools or tips on how to handle these changes, which led me down a hole of deep depression for a few months.

That was my first wake-up call. I realized I'd focused so much on moving forward that I forgot to check if I was moving in the right direction anymore. It was in that moment of clarity that I knew something had to change. The constant hustle, the never-ending chase for the next opportunity—it was all leading me nowhere. I started questioning what truly mattered to me, what kind of life I actually wanted to build. That realization set me on a path of self-discovery, where I slowly stepped away from the go-go-go mentality and began laying the foundation for something more meaningful, eventually leading me to start Simplending.

But I still hadn't truly learned how to pause. At one point while growing Simplending Financial, I found myself trapped in the illusion that busyness meant progress. I packed my schedule, answered emails deep into the night, and kept pushing under the belief that success was just one more effort away. But what I didn't see then was how fatigue was quietly working against me—shrinking my creativity, clouding my judgment, and shutting out the very breakthroughs I was chasing.

Today, some of my best decisions, my boldest ideas, and my most fruitful connections don't happen in a flurry of emails or during back-to-back meetings. They come during a walk when I step away from my desk. They come after I unplug for a weekend and let my mind wander. They come when I allow myself to be fully present instead of frantically checking tasks off a list.

In the world of entrepreneurship, hustle is often worn like a badge of honor. We glorify packed calendars, late nights, and the constant buzz of activity as proof that we're "doing the work." But exhaustion clouds our judgment. It narrows our vision. It makes us reactive instead of strategic.

What if the real power move isn't adding more to your plate but knowing when to step back?

Rest isn't a reward you earn after burning out; it's an essential business strategy. It's how we recharge our energy, refresh our creativity, and stay open to new ideas, partnerships, and opportunities that can't break through when we're running on empty.

When we rest, we're not stepping away from growth; we're stepping into it. We're trusting that sustainable success doesn't come from depleting ourselves but from maintaining the energy and clarity to lead effectively. True innovation, powerful partnerships, and inspired ideas don't thrive in a mind that's constantly fatigued. They emerge when we allow space for reflection, curiosity, and creativity.

This is a chapter about that pivotal moment we all need but rarely take: the pause.

In this chapter, you'll learn how to step back and embrace intentional pauses as a powerful tool for clarity, creativity, and sustainable success. You'll discover why taking time to rest and reflect isn't a sign of weakness but a proven strategy for making better decisions, staying focused on what matters, and avoiding burnout.

SCIENCE BEHIND PAUSING

Now, let's talk about what happens in your brain when you pause. Neuroscience research from Harvard Medical School has shown that with regular periods of deliberate pause, an area of our brains called the default mode network, or DMN, is activated.[1] Sometimes referred to as our "neural dark matter," this network plays a critical role in the following:

- Processing experiences
- Making sense of events

- Developing self-awareness

- Enhancing creativity

- Improving decision-making capabilities

A breakthrough finding from Princeton University's Neuroscience Institute further supports this. Scientists discovered that the brain needs time off to restart and maintain peak performance. These mental resets allow neural pathways to reroute, often leading to solutions for pressing challenges that would otherwise remain unclear if the mind were constantly running.[2]

A 2021 research study published in the *Clinical Psychology Review* found that those who took regular mindful pauses throughout their day showed a 43 percent improvement in decision-making quality, 37 percent less cortisol associated with stress, and a 28 percent increase in creative problem-solving skills.[3]

These are not just numbers but tangible benefits of something as simple as taking a moment to stop and breathe.

When I first came across this research, I was amazed. It completely shifted my perspective. I had spent years pushing forward, convinced that slowing down meant falling behind. But the science said otherwise.

I decided to experiment with intentional pauses—taking moments throughout my day to reset, breathe, and reflect. The impact was undeniable. My focus sharpened, my stress levels dropped, and for the first time in years, I felt in control rather than caught in an endless cycle of busyness.

MAKING TIME TO PAUSE

Building a company, leading a team, and innovating in a competitive market all require stamina. But stamina doesn't come from constant output;

it comes from intelligent energy management. Rest gives you the space to see opportunities you might otherwise miss. It allows you to respond thoughtfully instead of reacting impulsively. In fact, when you allow yourself structured downtime—real, quality rest—you often find that ideas you've been struggling with resolve themselves. Challenges start to seem more manageable. Solutions that felt out of reach suddenly come into view. Rest creates space for alignment, and alignment creates flow.

As I was building up two successful companies, I developed a number of important types of pauses that have been invaluable not only for myself but also for my employees. These help me step back, reassess, and stay aligned, even when I'm faced with challenges and difficult times.

The Morning Pause

This is your daily reset button. It's that quiet time before the world wakes up, when you can center yourself and set an intention for the day ahead. For me, that means twenty minutes of meditation followed by journal writing. It's about consistency, not duration.

The Strategic Pause

These are scheduled breaks during a segment of your workday, usually ten to fifteen minutes. They aren't for checking emails or scrolling mindlessly through social media. Take a step back, judge your progress, and realign your action, if necessary, toward your set goal.

The Emergency Pause

This is the circuit breaker when your emotions start to amplify or you feel overwhelmed by decisions. It's the three deep breaths you take before responding to that hard email or the walk around the block you take before making a huge business decision.

The Reflective Pause

This is where you will step back, usually on a weekly or monthly basis, to get a sense of the wider progress and make course corrections. I schedule these for every Sunday evening, creating space to review the past week and plan for the coming one.

WHEN PAUSING FEELS IMPOSSIBLE

Let me tell you about Sarah, one of my first clients at Simplending Financial. She came to me overwhelmed, running a growing real estate investment company that was consuming every minute of her day. I said, "Sarah, you have to carve out some time in your day and just sit and think." And she looked at me like I had told her to take up skydiving in the middle of her workday.

"I don't have much time to eat lunch as it is," she said. "How am I going to find time to stop?"

I smiled because I saw my former self in her resistance. I shared with her how my own resistance to pausing had almost derailed my success. It's quite true that the busier one gets, the more important it becomes to pause. You know, like trying to drive across the country without ever pulling in for gas: Sure enough, you'll eventually run out of fuel.

With Sarah, we started small—just three minutes of silence in the morning before she checked her phone. I had her do this at home, urging her to develop a habit in which she established her own mental tone before the demands of the world could take over. Those three

---

minutes gradually increased to five, then ten. After a few months, she called to say not only that she felt more grounded and present at work but that the biggest shift was evident in her decision-making. One example was a real estate investment that she had previously made without much deliberation. But this time, she stepped back.

Instead of succumbing to external pressure, she assessed the situation objectively and negotiated more favorable conditions. That one action resulted in a 40 percent increase in her revenue that year. She was convinced that it was because of the pauses.

USING THE PAUSE FRAMEWORK

Remember, every great journey starts with a single step—or in this case, a single pause. Trust the process, and watch as the simple act of stopping transforms not just your business but your entire approach to life. Each pause is a chance to reset your nervous system, realign with your purpose, reconnect with your intuitive wisdom, and remember what truly matters.

Your pauses will transition with you, and even if something works today, it may require modification tomorrow. Be curious or experimental. The impact of pause practice ripples so much further than your business's success—it hits every corner of your life and the lives of those around you.

I created the PAUSE acronym to help my clients remember key components of an effective pause:

Presence: Bring your entire attention into the present now.

Awareness: Observe your thoughts, feel your feelings, and sense all physical sensations.

Understanding: Reflect on what is essential now.

Stillness: Permit yourself to be at rest; it is receptive.

Emergence: Continue with clarity and insight into living.

Businesses today need leaders who can pause: leaders who know when to stop and have the courage to reflect and then the strength to go ahead with clarity and purpose.

I want you to take your first structured pause: Go to a quiet place, set a timer for three minutes, and just breathe. Observe your thoughts, but make no effort or attempt at changing them. At the end, jot down one insight or observation from the experience. This will be a beginning into the transformational power of the pause.

APPLYING THE PAUSE TO YOUR BUSINESS AND BUSINESS PLANS

Pausing is not only about personal well-being—it is a critical business tool. When integrated intentionally into your decision-making, planning, and leadership rhythm, it has the power to prevent costly mistakes, sharpen your strategy, and help you lead with clarity.

Pause Before Setting Goals

Before diving into a new quarter or launching a fresh campaign, step back and ask: What are we trying to accomplish and why? Too often, businesses set goals based on trends, pressure, or competitor activity rather than alignment with their deeper mission.

For example, a client running a successful online retail company came to me ready to expand into three new markets. Instead of rushing ahead, I encouraged her to schedule a two-day pause—no emails, no calls, just her, her leadership team, and a whiteboard. During this time, she revisited the company's core values and customer feedback.

The result? She decided to launch in only one market and invest the remaining budget into improving customer experience. Six months later, customer retention had grown by 31 percent.

Pause During Planning

A strategic plan is a guide, not a rule book. Before each major milestone, build in checkpoints to stop and assess: *Are we still on the right path? Has anything shifted?*

A midsize marketing agency I worked with used to jump from one project to another with little reflection. I introduced them to the "quarterly reflective pause"—a scheduled session where leadership reviewed what worked, what didn't, and what needed adjustment. This simple habit exposed inefficiencies, helped reallocate talent, and clarified priorities. Over time, team burnout dropped by 15 percent, and productivity rose by 10 percent.

Pause Before Making Key Decisions

When you're about to make a high-stakes decision such as hiring a new executive, pivoting your business model, or investing in a new tool, insert an emergency pause. Even ten minutes of silence can help clear the mental clutter and allow clarity to surface.

One of my financial clients was about to close on a multi-property deal. Everything looked good on paper. I encouraged him to step back and review the numbers again, without the broker or team present. In that pause, he noticed a miscalculation in projected maintenance costs that would've cut his return on investment (ROI) significantly. That pause saved him nearly $50,000.

Use the Reflective Pause for Long-Term Vision

The reflective pause isn't a luxury for when things are calm—it's a necessity for shaping the future. Schedule time at the end of each month or quarter to examine broader questions: *Where are we heading? What trends are emerging? What impact are we making?*

During one of my Sunday evening reviews, I realized that while both my companies were growing, my personal presence was shrinking. I was managing operations but losing connection with my mission. That insight led me to delegate more operational tasks and return to strategy, writing, and mentoring—areas where my impact was greatest.

Teach Your Team to Pause

Encourage your team members to adopt strategic, emergency, and reflective pauses in their workflows. One start-up founder I worked with introduced five-minute resets between internal meetings. Initially, her team resisted. But over time, they reported better focus, fewer miscommunications, and reduced meeting fatigue.

EMBRACING THE POWER OF STILLNESS

It takes courage and wisdom to take a break for yourself in a society that encourages busyness. The goal of pausing is to make space for greater impact, alignment, and clarity—not to stop making progress. When you incorporate deliberate periods of silence into your day, you invite new ideas, calm focus, and the kind of creativity that doesn't flourish in chaos. Whether it's a quiet moment in the morning, a deep breath before a big decision, or a reflective Sunday evening review, every pause becomes a reset button for your mind and your mission. It reminds you that your greatest breakthroughs rarely arrive when you're chasing everything at once. They show up when you slow down long enough to hear what really matters.

As you build the courage to stop, breathe, and be present, you create a wave of transformation that touches your team, your organization, your industry, and beyond.

REVIEW QUESTIONS

1. How did the author's early fast-paced lifestyle shape her understanding of the importance of pausing?

2. What major life events served as a wake-up call for the author to slow down and reassess her direction?

3. Why can busyness sometimes work against progress, especially in building a business?

4. According to neuroscience, what role does the DMN play when you pause?

5. What were some of the measurable benefits discovered in the 2021 *Clinical Psychology Review* study on mindful pauses?

6. What are the four types of pauses the author describes, and how does each serve a different purpose?

7. How did the author help Sarah integrate intentional pauses into her demanding workday, and what was the result?

8. What is the PAUSE framework, and how can it help you implement effective pauses?

9. How can pausing be applied practically to goal setting, planning, key decisions, and team culture within a business?

SHE RECEIVES:
GRATITUDE, FLOW, AND OVERFLOW

OPENING YOURSELF TO RECEIVE

From a young age, many women are taught—sometimes subtly, sometimes loudly—that their value is measured by how much they can give. We are praised for being "good daughters," "helpful friends," "supportive partners," and "selfless mothers." Our worth often becomes tangled up in how much we sacrifice, how available we are, and how much of ourselves we pour into others. Somewhere along the way, many of us learned that our needs should come last. That asking for help, accepting support, or celebrating our own wins is somehow selfish. Selflessness is often glorified like a badge of honor.

Think about it: How often are women celebrated not just for their achievements but for how much they endure? How often do we hear "She's so strong; she never asks for anything," or "She's amazing; she always puts everyone else first," "She sacrifices everything for her family," or "She works tirelessly behind the scenes"?

These are beautiful sentiments, until they become expectations. Until we are so emptied out from giving that there's nothing left for ourselves. The hidden cost of this unbalanced giving is burnout, resentment, and quiet sadness. A life half-lived because we were too busy serving to remember that we matter too.

And make no mistake: Giving is beautiful. Service is noble. Compassion is powerful. But when our giving becomes a requirement for feeling "enough," it turns into a quiet trap.

It's not your fault. It's the way the world has wired many of us to operate—that is, putting service on a pedestal while quietly whispering that receiving is indulgent or unnecessary.

There is a hidden side to this story of endless giving—a side we don't always talk about, but one that matters deeply. And today, we are rewriting that story. You were not created to be a machine of endless output. You were created to live, to love, to expand, and to receive just as much as you give.

And if we look even deeper, we start to see why so many women find giving easier—and safer—than receiving. When we give, we feel in control. We are the helpers, the fixers, the givers of comfort.

But when we receive? We have to open ourselves up. We have to be vulnerable. We have to trust that we are worthy of good things, without having to earn them through exhaustion or sacrifice.

Receiving asks us to believe that we are enough just as we are—and that can feel terrifying if we've spent a lifetime proving our worth through what we do for others. Receiving doesn't make you weak or selfish. It is a catalyst. It's the hidden element that transforms hard work into satisfaction and ambition into happiness.

There's a path where you can honor your generous heart and allow yourself to be poured into. Where you can give from overflow, not depletion. Where you can stand confidently in your right to receive every blessing, every opportunity, and every ounce of joy that's meant for you. It makes you whole.

In this chapter, you'll learn how to break free from the quiet belief that your worth depends only on how much you give. You'll explore why receiving is just as vital as giving—and how allowing yourself to receive love, help, opportunities, and blessings can replenish your energy, deepen your joy, and expand your impact.

THE SCIENCE OF RECEIVING

Opening yourself to receive is more than simply a "nice idea"; it's supported by science. Science is starting to understand what traditional wisdom has known for centuries: Giving and receiving are two sides of the same sacred loop, and balance is necessary for a vibrant, robust life.

A study published in *The Journal of Positive Psychology* discovered that those who practiced both giving and receiving reported better levels of well-being than those who just gave. Generosity felt great, but when participants let themselves accept support, gratitude, or compassion in exchange, their happiness, resilience, and sense of connection skyrocketed.[1]

Similarly, the *Harvard Business Review* found that responsive leaders—those who welcome feedback, collaboration, and support—build stronger teams and create more innovative environments.[2] These leaders are not just more effective at inspiring others; they are also more adaptive, inventive, and prepared to face obstacles. In other words, receiving is a leadership skill that promotes long-term success.

Allowing yourself to receive—whether it's a compliment, an opportunity, a helping hand, or unexpected abundance—replenishes your internal resources. You are communicating to your nervous system that it is safe to relax, be noticed, and excel. This generates a positive feedback loop that increases creativity, sharpens intuition, and attracts even more benefits to come your way.

By accepting the science of receiving, you give yourself permission to thrive—not just for a moment but over the long haul of your aspirations.

RECOGNIZING THE INVISIBLE BARRIERS TO RECEIVING

The fears that prevent us from receiving aren't always obvious. It's the small, everyday routines that seem so natural that we hardly notice them. We push ourselves to the limit without seeking any help. We downplay compliments with a quick, "Oh, it was nothing." We tell ourselves we'll slow down *after* the next project, *after* the next crisis, *after* everyone else's needs are met.

These minor acts of self-sabotage are not unintentional. They are survival mechanisms that we learned along the road, usually to keep ourselves from feeling vulnerable. We don't have to put up with the discomfort of being noticed if we keep ourselves busy. We avoid disappointment, betrayal, and feeling like a burden by rejecting praise or support. In our efforts to protect ourselves, we also close the door to abundance, joy, and deeper connection.

You need to be vulnerable to truly receive. Receiving requires us to be honest, visible, and acknowledge that we have needs and desires. And for many of us, especially women who were trained to value independence and self-sacrifice, this can be frightening. We somehow internalized a terrible myth: that power entails doing everything alone.

True strength, however, is not achieved alone. True strength is being capable of reaching out. It's understanding how to embrace love, support, and grace without reservation. It's recognizing that asking for help does not make you weak; rather, it makes you human.

When we associate strength with isolation, we not only exhaust ourselves but also cut ourselves off from the very flow of blessings that we seek. Connection leads to abundance. Success grows more quickly when it is nurtured by a village. When others observe the healing, it becomes more profound.

This is a lesson I learned firsthand. When I first started Simplending

Financial, I was fired up—passionate, driven, and determined to succeed. I invested everything I had into my financial venture: energy, expertise, and emotion. I was constantly on the move, fixing problems and assisting my team—doing everything. Initially, it appeared to be the only route forward. But beneath the momentum, a deep tiredness was rising, as was a latent anxiety that if I ever stopped, everything would come apart.

But sometime along the way, I realized something alarming. No matter how much we accomplished—new agreements closed, important milestones reached—I didn't feel the excitement or satisfaction I expected from achievement. I felt hollow. Restless. Already concerned about the next challenge to overcome.

It all came to a head the day we surpassed a massive deal volume milestone—something I had dreamed of since the beginning. I should have been celebrating. I should have been popping champagne and dancing in my office. But instead, I found myself skipping over it entirely, already obsessing about the next quarter's targets.

That moment stopped me in my tracks. I sat down, closed my eyes, and asked myself, *Why can't I just receive this moment?*

In that small, still space, something shifted. I whispered aloud, "You did this. You get to receive this." And for the first time in a long while, I let the accomplishment land. I felt my shoulders relax. My chest expanded with pride. Tears welled in my eyes—not from exhaustion but from genuine, soul-deep gratitude.

That moment was transformative. It taught me that receiving, like giving, is a practice. It requires intention. It requires presence. It needs you to give yourself permission to pause, breathe, and allow the good in.

From that day onward, I resolved to celebrate every victory, no matter how minor, allowing gratitude to fill the void that ambition previously occupied. And the more I practiced, the more energy, creativity, and flow I unleashed, not only for myself, but also for my entire team.

Acknowledgment helps anchor abundance.

Every time you take a moment to really appreciate the wonderful experiences you've created, you lay the groundwork for even more.

RELEASING GUILT, FEAR, AND SHAME AROUND RECEIVING

Receiving, for many women, is not only foreign but often uncomfortable. Even risky. Why? Because we were taught that love must be earned, worth must be demonstrated, and that shining too brightly attracts criticism, envy, or rejection.

Underneath the effort to receive is frequently a complex web of guilt, anxiety, and shame. Guilt over taking up space. Fear of being criticized or misunderstood. Shame for wanting more when others seem to have less. We often believe that we don't deserve something unless we work hard for it. *If I'm too successful, people will think I'm selfish. If I let it be easy, I must not be trying hard enough.*

But these stories are not the truth. They are old programs—survival mechanisms from a different time, passed down through generations. It is safe to release them. And we need to reframe success, so we feel safe to receive, shine, and to be seen in our fullness without shrinking, apologizing, or justifying.

Every time you allow yourself to receive love, praise, support, and abundance, you are rewriting those old scripts. You are creating a new reality where worthiness is not conditional and where thriving is your natural state.

Don't forget: Receiving is not a reward for perfection. It is your birthright.

TRUSTING THAT ABUNDANCE CAN COME WITH EASE

Many of us have quietly carried stories like *Success must be hard*, *Struggle makes me worthy*, and *If I don't suffer for it, it doesn't really count.*

This "struggle story" has a profound foundation. For decades, especially for women, survival necessitated tireless effort. Working harder, sacrificing more, and putting others first were all regarded as virtues or badges of honor.

However, your soul already understands that abundance does not require tiredness. Joy, flow, and alignment are strong—and often more sustainable—paths to success. When we let go of the assumption that everything must be gained through hard work, we open ourselves up to a kinder, more spacious way of life. We begin to believe that good things can come to us not because they are easy, but because we are finally at peace with life.

I encourage you to embrace these narratives: *My worth is not measured by exhaustion. I can be wildly successful while feeling peaceful and nourished. Struggle is not a prerequisite for receiving.*

When you live with ease, you naturally attract opportunities, support, and abundance. You're not swimming upstream anymore. You become an integral part of the river.

But how do we begin living this truth in everyday life? It starts with small, intentional rituals that honor ease and invite abundance.

PRACTICAL DAILY RITUALS TO ALIGN WITH EASE

Begin each day with five quiet minutes of stillness—just breathe and remind yourself that you are open to ease today. Throughout

continued

the day, pause for gratitude check-ins, shifting your focus from chasing the future to appreciating the present moment. Sprinkle in micro-joy wherever you can: Dance for a few minutes, step into the sunlight, or share a laugh with a friend—these small bursts of joy redirect your energy toward receiving. When faced with decisions, pause before saying yes and ask yourself whether it feels aligned or simply obligated. Let your sense of ease be your compass. The more you intentionally weave ease into your daily rhythm, the more natural it becomes to receive—without guilt, apology, or resistance. You do not have to suffer to succeed.

RECEIVING SUPPORT AS A LEADERSHIP SKILL

Imagine this: A team leader is preparing for a major presentation. Instead of taking on every task alone, she invites her team members to contribute. One colleague with strong design skills enhances the visuals, another helps research key stats, and a third rehearses with her. On presentation day, she's not drained—she's energized. She steps into the room grounded, confident, and fully present.

Many women have been taught at some point in their lives that leadership entails carrying the world alone. That "real strength" looks like never asking for help, doing everything on your own, and holding it all together with no cracks, no weakness, and no needs.

True leadership, however, is more than just being a lone warrior; it's about forging connections, inspiring others, and allowing support to spread.

Receiving help sends a powerful and empowering message to others watching: I don't have to do it all alone, and neither should you. When you receive, you exemplify permission. You demonstrate that collaboration is strength, not weakness. You cultivate a culture in which asking, receiving, and interdependence are valued rather than shamed. And you increase your energy.

This is the power of receiving: It shifts us from burnout to brilliance. When you're nourished, your vision sharpens, your creativity expands, and your impact grows.

TRUSTING YOUR TEAM

One of my clients, a founder of a community-based organization, once shared how receiving transformed her leadership. In the early years, she wore every hat, managing logistics, fundraising, events, and mentoring. Eventually, her passion began to fade. When she finally began trusting her core team to take ownership of key roles, everything changed.

Team morale rose as members felt genuinely trusted and empowered to lead. No longer micromanaged, they became more engaged, confident, and proud of their contributions.

The quality of work noticeably improved. With responsibilities shared, tasks were completed with greater focus and creativity. Each person brought their unique strengths, leading to higher standards and fresh ideas.

Freed from the constant pressure of doing it all, she found herself thinking more clearly and creatively. This new space allowed her to step into her role as a visionary leader—present, strategic, and deeply connected to her mission.

As a result, the organization began to flourish. It was no longer reliant on one person's effort but driven by a collaborative, energized team where support and innovation flowed freely.

By receiving support, she didn't lose control; she gained momentum. And so did everyone around her.

ACCEPTING SUPPORT BUILDS TRUST

Receiving support entails more than simply saying yes when offered assistance; it entails truly trusting others to share their skills, ideas, and strength.

Instead of clinging to control—*If I don't do it, it won't be right*—leadership encourages you to embrace empowerment—*I can trust others to rise and shine*. Micromanagement drains. Empowerment energizes. Receiving elevates leadership from a burden to a collaborative, dynamic force.

Can you guess the ripple effect? Every time you gracefully receive, you make room for someone else to contribute from their own fullness. You activate their capabilities. You recognize their contribution. You let generosity flow in both directions.

Receiving is a catalyst. It improves the overall ecosystem around you. You were not meant to undertake this adventure alone. You are part of a larger web that is active, linked, and thriving.

Let receiving be your leadership superpower. Make it a present to yourself—and everyone else.

WHEN RECEIVING TRIGGERS OLD WOUNDS

It's very easy for me to encourage you to be open to receiving help, but for many of us, receiving feels unsafe. The moment you start to open yourself to receive, something unexpected may happen: A quiet voice from the past may rise within you, telling you that you don't deserve it.

This is too much.

You're not worthy of this attention, this praise, this help.

And this discomfort isn't just a passing feeling; it's rooted in old wounds, long-held stories, and deep-seated beliefs we carry about ourselves.

If someone broke your trust in the past, whether through betrayal, abandonment, or unfulfilled promises, the instinct to guard yourself becomes a reflex. Perhaps you confided in someone you considered a close friend, only to have them share your private story with others. Or maybe you relied on a partner to show up during a crisis, and they didn't show up.

These moments leave a residue: *It's safer if I just handle things on my own.*

The very act of receiving, of opening up to the possibility of support, may trigger a fear that it will be withdrawn, mishandled, or used against you. Receiving feels like risking more hurt.

And that fear is real. It's valid. But it doesn't have to control you.

HEALING THE RECEIVING WOUND

Imagine that you are leading a big project at work. A colleague offers to help—not because you can't do it but because they admire your work and want to support you. Instinctively, you feel tension rise in your body. You know you could do it all yourself. You've done it alone before. And if you hand over this task to your colleague, what if they mess it up? What if they do it poorly and it reflects poorly on you?

But what if you let them help you instead of doing it alone? What if you gave them clear guidance and then trusted them to contribute? What if the gift wasn't just their help but also the courage it took to receive it?

Healing happens when you choose to lean into the discomfort, not run from it. When you allow yourself to receive, even in the face of fear, you reclaim your power to trust again.

Healing isn't about rushing to feel better; it's about giving yourself the space to mend. Here are some steps you can take to gently begin healing your wounds:

- Start small.

- Accept compliments.

- Let someone help you with a simple task.

- Give yourself permission to enjoy a moment of success—without guilt.

Each time you let your guard down a little bit and receive, you send a message to your subconscious that it is safe to trust again. And the more you practice, the less power these old wounds will have over you.

HOLDING YOURSELF WITH COMPASSION THROUGH DISCOMFORT

Because of these past wounds, you might not always feel "ready" to receive. You might feel nervous, hesitant, or even guilty. But here's the key: Show up for yourself in those moments, with compassion.

Acknowledge the discomfort. *I see you, fear. I understand why you're here, but I choose to receive anyway.* In those moments, you practice self-compassion and kindness. Remember, healing isn't linear. There will be times when the fear rises, when the old wounds ache. But the more you choose to receive, to trust yourself and others, the more you heal.

You are worthy of receiving, even when it feels hard—especially when it feels hard.

PRACTICAL EXERCISES FOR OPENING TO RECEIVING

Opening yourself up to receive is a path that involves practice, patience, and intention. It is not something that occurs overnight. But every step, no matter how tiny, brings you closer to a life in which receiving is as natural as giving.

Practice Daily "Receiving Reflection"

At the close of each day, take a minute to reflect and list three things you allowed yourself to receive. It could be as simple as taking a compliment, having someone hold the door open for you, or accepting assistance with a chore. The trick is to acknowledge what you have received, no matter how insignificant it may appear.

This exercise trains your mind to recognize the abundance that surrounds you and helps you focus on what you're willing to receive rather than what you're holding back. Over time, you'll realize how much love, support, and kindness are always available to you.

Practice Saying "Thank You" Without Deflection When Praised

How often do you reject compliments?

"Thank you, but I couldn't have done it without my team."

"Thank you, but it was really just luck."

"Thank you, but there's always more work to be done."

While these reactions may appear humble, they can impede the flow of receiving. The next time someone compliments you or recognizes your accomplishments, simply say "Thank you" without qualifications, explanations, or self-deprecation. You deserve to be praised, and taking praise graciously invites more positivity and abundance into your life.

Set Small Goals to Ask for and Accept Support Weekly

Many of us have been raised to be self-sufficient and do everything on our own. True strength, however, lies in having the courage to seek assistance and accept support from others. Set small, manageable goals and actively seek help from others. It might be asking a coworker for assistance with a project, asking a friend to run an errand, or even seeking emotional support while feeling overwhelmed.

Begin with one request per week.

Remember that getting support does not make you weak; rather, it empowers you. The more you practice asking for and receiving help, the easier it becomes and the more you allow people to step into their own power.

THE GIFT OF RECEIVING

Throughout this chapter, we've unwrapped a powerful truth: You were never meant to pour endlessly from an empty cup. Your needs matter. Your joy matters. Your ability to receive support, love, and ease isn't a luxury; it's part of your leadership, your abundance, and your wholeness.

This is your permission slip to stop striving to "earn" your worth through endless giving. You can build, lead, and love from a place of fullness, where your energy renews instead of depletes, where your spirit expands instead of contracts. You are already enough. So today, what if you let yourself receive—a compliment, a helping hand, a quiet moment of peace—without apology? You're not just making your own life richer. You're lighting the way for others to do the same.

Let's keep rewriting this story together.

REVIEW QUESTIONS

1. Why is endless giving often glorified, especially for women, and what are the hidden costs?

2. How does exhaustion affect decision-making, creativity, and leadership?

3. How does the belief that "receiving is selfish" impact women's leadership and personal fulfillment?

4. How can receiving support be seen as an act of strength in leadership rather than weakness?

5. Why is it important to model receiving support for the people around you?

6. What does it mean to lead from abundance rather than depletion?

7. In what ways can practicing ease daily help you shift into a more abundant mindset?

8. What are some small, practical rituals suggested to realign with ease every day?

9. How does celebrating micro-joys help open you up to a flow of ease and receiving?

10. After reading this chapter, what is one area in your life where you will intentionally begin practicing receiving?

CHAPTER 15

CULTIVATING GRATITUDE, EVEN IN CHALLENGING TIMES

It is not joy that makes us grateful;
it is gratitude that makes us joyful.
—DAVID STEINDL-RAST

About a year after launching Simplending Financial, just when I thought we were beginning to gain real momentum, in the span of a single week, three major deals fell through, collectively worth over $750,000 in projected revenue.

One was a partnership with a regional bank that would have expanded our lending network significantly and was valued at close to $300,000 over the first year. Another was a corporate client we had spent months courting, who ultimately decided to work with a larger firm, an opportunity that could've brought in around $200,000. The third was a funding agreement worth roughly $250,000 that collapsed at the final stages due to unforeseen regulatory changes.

The weight of it was crushing—three huge opportunities lost, and the future suddenly seemed uncertain. The panic started to set in, and I could feel the stress creeping in. It would have been easy to spiral, to let the frustration and disappointment consume me. But I turned to my gratitude practice. I wrote down the things I was thankful for that day, despite the setbacks.

"Grateful for the lessons these deals brought." "Grateful for the incredible team navigating the storm with me." "Grateful for the belief that what's meant for us won't miss us."

Those few words on paper changed everything. Instead of panic, I felt a calm clarity wash over me. I could see the situation for what it was—an inevitable part of the entrepreneurial journey. The shift wasn't immediate, but it was powerful. Gratitude helped me stay grounded and focused on what truly mattered: the bigger picture, the long-term vision, and the people around me who believed in what we were building.

Every single day, no matter how hard the journey felt, I made it a point to reflect on the things I was grateful for—both big and small. Some days, I was thankful for a successful client meeting or a milestone reached in the business. Other days, it was as simple as appreciating a quiet cup of coffee before sunrise or the encouraging words from a mentor or friend. It was this simple act of recognizing the blessings—whether monumental or modest—that helped me stay focused, motivated, and, most importantly, resilient.

Gratitude became my anchor. It boosted my ability to recover from failures, to persevere in the face of adversity, and to see each obstacle as a stepping stone to something better. This shaped me as a person. The more I practiced gratitude, the more I noticed it sparked growth, success, and deeper fulfillment.

As entrepreneurs, we usually face setbacks in our business—moments of triumph followed by periods of struggle. In those difficult times, it's easy to get overwhelmed, lose sight of the bigger picture, or to spiral into doubt. But when you decide to lead with gratitude, something changes:

You begin to see opportunities instead of obstacles, growth instead of setbacks, and strength instead of fragility. Gratitude is a transformative tool that has the power to change your mindset, business, and life.

In this chapter, you'll learn how gratitude can help you become more resilient and grow as a person. You not only create a business but also a life you love when you include gratitude in your entrepreneurial endeavors.

GRATITUDE AS A TOOL FOR GRACE IN TOUGH TIMES

As an entrepreneur, it's easy to focus on the things that aren't working: the deals that fell through, the obstacles you didn't anticipate, the endless to-do list that never seems to shrink. You may not always have control over the outcomes, but you always have control over how you choose to respond.

Gratitude shifts your focus from panic to grace. It invites you to step back and reflect on what you've already accomplished, the lessons you've learned, and the people who have supported you along the way. It's a practice that refuels your energy when you're running on empty, and it helps you appreciate the small wins just as much as the big ones.

Gratitude is the choice to see the silver lining in the midst of a difficult project. The choice to acknowledge your growth, even when the finish line feels far away. Gratitude empowers you to respond with a sense of grace, optimism, and purpose, no matter what's happening around you. It doesn't mean saying "thank you" when things go right—it's about cultivating a mindset that allows you to see the value in every moment, every challenge, and every step of the journey.

It reminds you that growth isn't linear; it's messy and complicated, and it often requires us to pivot. But gratitude allows you to embrace that messiness, to appreciate the journey as much as the destination. It's a practice that reminds you of your purpose, keeps you grounded amid chaos, and helps you maintain perspective when the road gets tough. Gratitude, in the entrepreneurial sense, is a tool for resilience.

HOW GRATITUDE BUILDS RESILIENCE

When you think of gratitude, you might imagine it as a feel-good concept—something that makes you smile and feel warm inside. But what if I told you that gratitude is more than just a nice thought? It's backed by science and has the power to physically and emotionally transform your life, especially as an entrepreneur navigating the highs and lows of building something from scratch.

Dr. Robert Emmons, one of the world's leading experts on gratitude, has spent decades researching its effects. His studies reveal something profound: Gratitude boosts your mood, strengthens your immune system, lowers blood pressure, and increases your overall optimism.[1] Imagine having these physical and emotional benefits working for you, especially when things get tough. As an entrepreneur, stress has become a familiar companion—one I've had to learn to navigate rather than avoid.

The emotional resilience that gratitude fosters is priceless. Resilience is the ability to bounce back from adversity, and for entrepreneurs, it's essential. Challenges come with the territory—whether it's a deal falling through, a team issue, or the pressure of juggling multiple tasks. But gratitude helps you weather these storms with a level head and a clear heart. Instead of feeling overwhelmed by the setbacks, gratitude shifts your perspective, allowing you to see the lesson in each challenge and the opportunity for growth.

When you pause and shift your focus to what you are grateful for, it has a way of bringing you back to a place of calm. It empowers you to keep going with a sense of purpose, knowing that setbacks are just part of the process. Gratitude isn't about denying the hard moments; it's about choosing to see the good that still exists within them.

That shift from panic to grace is the emotional resilience that every entrepreneur needs to survive—and thrive. Gratitude doesn't just help you push through the tough times; it transforms how you experience them. Instead of feeling defeated, you start to see every challenge as an opportunity to grow stronger. And in the world of entrepreneurship, that mindset is everything.

LEADING WITH GRATITUDE TO SHAPE COMPANY CULTURE

Gratitude is a personal practice and a powerful leadership tool that can shape the entire culture of your company. When you lead with gratitude, it creates a ripple effect that extends far beyond your own mindset. It affects the energy, morale, and trust within your team, turning your workplace into a space where people want to contribute and collaborate.

If there's one thing I picked up quickly while building Simplending Financial, it's that gratitude is the energy you show up with—the way you lead, the way you connect. As a leader, the energy you radiate is contagious. If you lead with appreciation, recognition, and a genuine sense of gratitude, your team will follow suit. They'll feel valued, seen, and motivated to give their best, knowing that their hard work is being noticed.

It wasn't just about what I did but how I did it. Whether it was thanking a team member for their late-night effort on a project, celebrating small wins along the way, or simply acknowledging my team's everyday contributions, gratitude became a cornerstone of how I led. This was particularly important when the going got tough. During those times when we faced setbacks, I made sure to highlight the effort and resilience of the team rather than dwelling on the challenges. It's easy to focus on what's going wrong—but focusing on what's going right is the key to keeping morale up.

And it wasn't just my team that felt the impact of this gratitude. Clients could feel the positive energy too. There's something magnetic about a company that leads with appreciation and respect. People want to be around that energy—it's inspiring. Gratitude within the company translated to better relationships with clients, because when you're genuinely appreciative of the people you work with, they feel valued. And when clients feel valued, they're more likely to remain loyal, refer others, and stick with you through the ups and downs of the business journey.

The culture of gratitude also had a profound effect on how clients interacted with us. They could sense the positive energy from our team, and it made them feel confident that they were working with a company that genuinely cared. When gratitude flows through your company, it attracts people who resonate with that energy: clients, partners, and employees alike. It becomes a magnet for those who value trust, respect, and collaboration. And as any entrepreneur knows, that's the kind of energy that leads to long-term success.

LEADING WITH GRATITUDE TO BUILD TRUST AND MORALE

Gratitude also improves morale and builds trust inside your company. When you consistently show appreciation and recognition, you're demonstrating that you value people beyond what they can do for you. It's not transactional; it's relational. This creates a deeper bond between you and your team, fostering loyalty and commitment. People don't just show up for the paycheck—they show up because they believe in what you're doing and feel personally invested in the company's success.

Honestly, it was amazing to watch how much things started to shift after I made gratitude a daily, intentional part of my leadership. It was something I modeled openly in team meetings, one-on-ones, and client interactions. I integrated it into how I communicated, made decisions, and celebrated progress. Over time, this shifted the energy in the company. It became part of our culture.

Our team became more cohesive, more willing to go above and beyond, and more connected to the vision we were building. They knew that their efforts were making a difference in helping our clients regain financial clarity, reduce debt, and achieve goals they once thought were out of reach. For many of our clients, we were offering service, peace of mind, confidence, and the ability to dream again. That's what made the work so meaningful; it was about being part of something bigger and delivering results.

So, if you want to build a team that thrives, a client base that trusts you, and a company culture that people can't wait to be a part of, lead with gratitude. It's a simple yet transformative tool that will help you create an environment where everyone feels valued, motivated, and ready to contribute. And in the end, that's what will drive your business forward.

ROOTING YOUR GRATITUDE IN PURPOSE

At the core of every thriving business is a sense of purpose. Do you remember the chapter on pursuing your purpose? That's the reason you created this business in the first place: to serve, to solve real problems, and to make a difference in people's lives. But here's the thing: Purpose goes beyond what you do. It's also about why you do it. And gratitude plays a key role in this. When you're grateful for the opportunities, the lessons, and the people around you, it fuels a deeper connection to your mission. You stop chasing success for the sake of success itself and start chasing it because it aligns with your values, your passions, and your bigger vision for the world.

In my journey building Simplending Financial, I realized that the more I leaned into gratitude, the more aligned I felt with my purpose, which is to provide honest, accessible, and empowering financial solutions that help individuals and families take control of their finances, break free from debt, and build a more secure and confident future. Sure, there were moments where I wondered if the sacrifices were worth it or if the late nights would ever pay off. But gratitude gave me clarity. It reminded me that each step, even the small ones, brought me closer to creating something that mattered—not just for me but for the people I served. It allowed me to see the bigger picture and understand that success goes beyond hitting sales targets or growing the number of clients. It's also about making a meaningful impact.

Gratitude is a foundational tool for long-term growth and true satisfaction, both in business and in life. It's the secret ingredient that, when consistently practiced, nurtures your mindset, fuels your purpose, and helps you create a life that's not only successful but deeply fulfilling.

And it doesn't stop at business. Gratitude isn't something that just stays within the four walls of your office or the confines of your workday. It has this incredible ripple effect that extends into your personal life, too. When you practice gratitude regularly, it shifts your entire perspective on the world. It affects the way you show up in relationships, how you handle challenges, and even how you view your own personal growth. You begin to appreciate the little moments—the quiet morning with a cup of coffee, the time spent with loved ones, the progress you've made, no matter how small.

For me, gratitude has reshaped how I interact with people. It's helped me appreciate the relationships I've built along the way and not take them for granted. It's reminded me that true fulfillment doesn't come from ticking boxes on a to-do list—it comes from the connections we make and the positive impact we have on others.

This ripple effect of gratitude has had a profound influence on my overall life satisfaction. It's not just about celebrating milestones or accomplishments; it's about appreciating the journey, even when things aren't perfect. And when you embrace gratitude as a proactive tool, you start to shape a life that feels meaningful, balanced, and rewarding, long after the initial excitement of success has faded.

So, I encourage you to make gratitude more than just a reaction to good things. Make it a habit, a mindset, and a foundation for everything you do. When you cultivate gratitude, you create the space to grow—not just as an entrepreneur but as a person. It will guide you through the tough times, inspire your team, and build a life you can look back on and be proud of. One that's defined by purpose, fulfillment, and meaningful connections.

HOW TO INTEGRATE GRATITUDE INTO YOUR DAILY LIFE

If you're wondering where to begin, here are some meaningful ways you can weave gratitude into your day, even with a packed schedule.

Client and Team Acknowledgments

Every week, make it a point to send a quick thank-you email to a client who trusted you with their business or a team member who went the extra mile. It doesn't have to be formal or scripted—just a simple, genuine note of appreciation. Not only does this strengthen relationships, but it also keeps you connected to the real people behind your business's success.

Here's a simple example of a thank-you email you might send:

SUBJECT: THANK YOU FOR TRUSTING US

Hi [Client's Name],

I just wanted to personally thank you for choosing Simplending Financial to support your business goals. We truly appreciate the trust you've placed in us, and we're committed to delivering results that help you succeed. Working with visionary clients like you reminds us why we do what we do.

If there's ever anything more we can do to support you, don't hesitate to reach out.

Wishing you continued success,

[Your Name]

Or if it's for a team member:

SUBJECT: GRATEFUL FOR YOUR HARD WORK

Hi [Team Member's Name],

I just wanted to take a moment to recognize and thank you for your incredible work on [specific project or task]. Your dedication and attention to detail didn't go unnoticed, and it made a real difference.

I'm so grateful to have you as part of the team. Keep shining—you're making an impact!

Warmly,

[Your Name]

Build a "Win Wall"

Create a space, whether it's a physical board, a digital folder, or even a section in your notes app, where you track every success, big or small. Signed a new partnership? Add it. Got a glowing client review? Add it. Overcame a tough challenge? That counts too. Over time, your "win wall" becomes a visual celebration of your journey and a reminder of how capable you are, especially on hard days.

A compelling real-world example of an entrepreneur who practices the "win wall" concept is Michael Dill, a certified business coach with ActionCOACH. During his quarterly strategic planning sessions, with groups of thirty-five to fifty business owners, Dill incorporates a "win wall" activity.[2] In this exercise, each participant writes down their recent achievements on Post-it notes and shares them with the group before placing them on a designated wall. This practice fosters a culture of recognition and positivity and also reinforces the importance of celebrating progress, both big and small, within a business setting. Dill emphasizes that acknowledging these wins can boost morale and set a productive tone for the upcoming quarter, helping business owners enter the next phase of planning with renewed confidence and momentum.

At Simplending Financial, we've adopted a similar approach. We don't use a physical wall, but we take time during team meetings to highlight individual and collective wins, whether it's a successfully closed client case, an act of outstanding teamwork, or a personal milestone. This consistent practice has helped strengthen team morale, encouraged a culture of appreciation, and kept everyone motivated by reminding us of how far we've come—even amid challenges.

Start Meetings with Wins

Bring gratitude into your leadership meetings. Begin every meeting by asking everyone to share one recent win or one thing they're proud of, whether it's a work-related achievement or personal milestone. It sets a positive tone, boosts morale, and reminds everyone that, even in a fast-paced environment, progress is happening. At Simplending Financial, this simple habit has become a core part of our team culture. Whether it's helping a client reach a financial milestone or someone tackling a personal goal, acknowledging these wins keeps us connected to our purpose and energized for what's ahead.

A notable real-world example of an entrepreneur who integrates gratitude into leadership meetings is Patrick Collison, CEO of Stripe.[3] He has implemented a practice where every other week, a customer joins the first thirty minutes of Stripe's leadership meetings to share positive feedback. This approach fosters a culture of appreciation and keeps the team connected to the real-world impact of their work. Collison notes that, despite having various feedback channels, this practice consistently inspires new insights.

Celebrate Financial Milestones—No Matter the Size

In the financial world, it's easy to focus only on the big wins—major contracts signed, revenue goals crushed. But celebrating smaller financial milestones like improving cash flow, securing a new referral partner, or even successfully renegotiating vendor terms keeps momentum high and builds confidence within your team. At Simplending Financial, we make it a point to acknowledge these moments in our team meetings, group chats, or through a quick shout-out. This practice reminds everyone that progress comes in many forms and reinforces the value of each person's contribution, no matter how small it may seem.

Practice Gratitude When Facing Challenges

Instead of only being grateful when things are going well, challenge yourself to find the silver lining when things don't go as planned. Maybe a deal fell through but taught you a valuable lesson. Maybe a slow month gave you time to streamline your systems. Acknowledging growth opportunities, even in setbacks, builds real resilience.

At Simplending, there was a period when a key partnership unexpectedly ended, which initially felt like a major blow. But that gap pushed us to diversify our referral sources and led to the development of a stronger, more reliable lead pipeline—something we might not have prioritized otherwise.

End the Week with a Gratitude Review

Before you close your laptop on Friday, take five minutes to reflect: What went well this week? What conversations energized you? What progress, however small, did you make? Ending your week this way helps you step into your weekend with pride and sets a strong, positive mindset for the week ahead. At Simplending, we've made this a habit by having each team member share one win and one moment of gratitude during our Friday wrap-up call—it's a simple practice that keeps morale high and helps us end the week on an encouraging note.

Now, I want to challenge you: For the next month, commit to writing down three things you're grateful for each day. Just three. They can be big or small, and they can come from any part of your life—work, family, health, nature, anything. At the end of the month, take some time to reflect on how this practice has shifted your perspective. How does your mindset feel now? Are you more resilient in the face of challenges? Have you noticed a deeper sense of joy or connection in your daily life?

Take a moment today to pause, reflect, and give thanks for the good things in your life. And remember, it's the small, consistent actions that create big shifts over time. Gratitude is a habit that has the power to transform. By making it a daily practice, you're not just changing your mindset—you're changing your life.

LET GRATITUDE LEAD THE WAY

Gratitude is a transformative tool that can reshape not only your business but your entire life. Whether you're an entrepreneur navigating the highs and lows of building a company or someone facing challenges along your journey, gratitude has the power to turn obstacles into opportunities and setbacks into lessons. It shifts your mindset, elevates your resilience, and fuels your ability to stay grounded through even the toughest moments.

When I reflect on my own journey, I realize that gratitude has been a constant companion. From the sleepless nights to the tough decisions, gratitude has kept me focused, grounded, and motivated. It's been my source of strength through the uncertainties of building Simplending Financial and my source of joy through the small victories and everyday blessings. Gratitude has illuminated my path—not just as a business owner but as a person living a fuller, more meaningful life.

The beauty of gratitude is that it doesn't just lead to business success—it leads to a life you love. By embracing gratitude, you're not just building a business or achieving goals; you're cultivating a sense of purpose, fulfillment, and connection in everything you do. You're inviting joy into your life, and when you do that, the ripple effect is profound. Your relationships improve, your perspective shifts, and you begin to see opportunities where you once saw roadblocks.

I want to leave you with this: Take action today. Start your own gratitude practice, no matter how small. Write down three things you're grateful for every day. Take a moment to pause, reflect, and appreciate the good in your life. Watch how these simple acts transform your mindset, your business, and your life.

Remember, it's the cornerstone of a life you love. Begin now, and watch the miracles unfold.

REVIEW QUESTIONS

1. How did practicing gratitude help the author during the early days of building Simplending Financial?

2. What are some examples of small moments the author chose to be grateful for during challenging times?

3. Why is gratitude described as a transformative tool for entrepreneurs?

4. In what ways can gratitude shift your perspective during periods of struggle?

5. How does daily gratitude impact resilience and motivation?

6. In your own words, how can intentionally integrating gratitude into daily routines shape your growth as a leader?

7. What is one simple way to practice gratitude toward clients or team members each week?

8. Why is it important to keep gratitude notes genuine and personal rather than formal and scripted?

9. How does expressing appreciation strengthen professional relationships?

10. What does the sample thank-you email to a client emphasize about building trust?

CHAPTER 16

GIVING FROM OVERFLOW

When a woman finally learns that pleasing the world is
impossible, she becomes free to learn how to please herself.
—GLENNON DOYLE

When we talk about success, certain things come to mind: a business that is doing well, a dream home, being financially free. I've learned along the way, though, that real success is more than just what you build for yourself; real success is overflowing. It creates opportunities, opens doors, and lifts others. It gives back to your community—through empowerment, resources, and shared growth.

I will never forget the day a young businesswoman walked into my office—nervous but determined—clutching a folder with a rough business plan and a heart full of hope. She had been turned away from multiple lenders, told her vision was "too ambitious" and "not practical." But as I sat across from her, I didn't just see the numbers or gaps in her pitch. I saw drive, resilience, and the spark of something extraordinary waiting to unfold if someone would simply believe in her. That conversation shifted something in me. I realized I didn't just want to help people grow wealth; I wanted to help them rebuild confidence, restore hope, and rewrite the narratives they had been handed. That encounter became the quiet heartbeat of everything I would later build. Giving back wasn't going to be an afterthought; it was going to be the mission.

From the very beginning of my entrepreneurial journey, when I sat down to plan what would eventually become Simplending Financial, I knew I wanted it to be exceptional. I envisioned a platform where people could be empowered and where success wasn't just measured by money but by impact. It wasn't something we would do to mark off that we had "made it." For us, it was baked into the foundation and sewn into our very being. Through accessible loans, we aim to give our clients the tools to build businesses, support their families, and transform their futures.

Because here's the beautiful thing: When you pour into others, you don't lose anything; you actually create more. More growth. More connection. More abundance. Giving back creates a cycle—a ripple effect—that multiplies far beyond anything you could achieve alone.

We began Chapter 14 exploring the art of receiving—learning to accept support, rest, and abundance without guilt. But here's the truth: Receiving and giving aren't opposites—they're part of the same flow. When you learn to receive well, you become more able to give from a place of fullness, not depletion. You stop giving out of obligation and start giving from overflow.

This chapter is about that magic. It's about how giving back doesn't just change someone else's life—it transforms yours, too.

In this chapter, you'll learn how true generosity flows not from obligation but from a life filled first. You'll see why giving back should never drain you but instead multiply your impact, your joy, and your community's growth.

GIVING BACK CREATES ABUNDANCE

One of the greatest lessons I've learned—and continue to witness every single day—is this: Giving back doesn't deplete you; it expands you.

For a long time, there's been this quiet belief floating around that giving means you have less. Less time. Less energy. Less money. That somehow, when you give, you're slicing up your own pie and handing out the pieces until you're left with crumbs.

And for many women, that belief has been reinforced by a culture that *expects* them to give endlessly—to care, to serve, to sacrifice—often without recognition or replenishment. That kind of giving is rooted in obligation, and yes, it can be exhausting. But here's what I've discovered through real experience: Giving doesn't divide—it multiplies.

The giving I'm talking about here is different. It's intentional. It's empowered. It flows from wholeness, not guilt. It's the kind of giving that's aligned with purpose and vision, where you choose to pour into others because you're also pouring into yourself. When you pour into someone else—whether it's sharing your knowledge, opening a door, making a connection, or offering encouragement—you're not just giving *them* something; you're also expanding your own capacity. You're growing your leadership, deepening your fulfillment, and strengthening the community around you.

And when *they* grow? When *they* rise? They go on to lift others too. It's a ripple effect that turns into a wave. And before you know it, the impact is bigger than anything you could have achieved alone.

At Simplending Financial, we've seen it firsthand. A woman we mentored eventually became a leader who now runs workshops for aspiring entrepreneurs. A young man who attended one of our free events went on to launch a nonprofit that now teaches financial literacy to underserved youth. One seed. One conversation. One moment of belief. And the ripple just keeps moving outward, touching lives we may never even meet.

Giving back isn't subtraction. It's *amplification*. It's multiplication. It's the secret ingredient that turns success into significance. That's the cycle of abundance. It's a beautiful, unstoppable force where generosity fuels growth, and growth fuels more generosity.

So if you've ever hesitated to give back—thinking you're too small, too busy, not ready yet—let me encourage you: You have something to give right now. And when you give from a place of wholeness, purpose, and abundance, you're not losing anything. You're stepping into a bigger, richer, more meaningful version of your life. You're building capacity for miracles you haven't even imagined yet.

BUILDING A COMPANY WHERE GIVING BACK IS THE HEARTBEAT

In the early days of my career, I worked with investment firms and financial institutions where I was involved in structuring deals, analyzing portfolios, and advising clients on strategic growth. It was a fast-paced environment that sharpened my skills but often felt disconnected from real people and real impact. I had spent enough time in boardroom meetings where the only things that were relevant were bottom lines and quarterly reports. I knew I wanted something different—something that would stand the test of time because it was rooted in purpose, not necessarily profit. From day one, giving back wasn't treated like an extracurricular activity we would get around to "someday." It was, and still is, at the center of everything we do.

It shows up in the way we mentor new recruits, in the programs we offer to empower women entering the financial sector, in the workshops we host to make real estate literacy accessible to everyone, not just the already connected. Giving back isn't a department or a committee; it's the heartbeat of Simplending.

It's ingrained into our work culture, our discussions, and the way we define success. Around here, winning does not imply standing alone at the top. It means bringing as many people with you as possible.

Mentorship: Planting Seeds for the Next Generation

I will never forget a young woman I met in a break room just after our leadership workshop I had hosted for junior staff. She lingered behind, nervously twisting her notebook in her hands, before quietly asking me, "Do you really think there's room for someone like me here?" I didn't hesitate. I said, locking eyes with her, "Not only is there room, we are building the table."

That conversation ignited a deeper commitment in me. It wasn't enough to be successful personally; I had a responsibility to create real pathways for others. That personal connection inspired us to take action on a broader scale. We invested time into creating leadership pipelines, shadowing opportunities, and small-group mentorship circles where goals were celebrated, not scoffed at. Watching assistants rise into leadership roles, seeing once-hesitant voices now commanding rooms with confidence—there's nothing more rewarding. That's the power of giving back to the next generation.

Mentorship has proven to be one of the most successful methods for me to give back. There is something incredibly moving about sitting across from someone who reminds you of your younger self—full of dreams, potential, and a thousand questions they are almost too scared to ask.

THE SCIENCE BEHIND GIVING: WHY IT CHANGES YOU, TOO

Apart from the obvious benefits of empowering others, giving back has a positive impact on you as well. It's more than simply a "nice thing to do"; it's a life-changing experience.

According to neuroscientific research, when we engage in acts of generosity, such as mentoring someone, sharing knowledge, or simply being kind to others, our brains actually light up. The same reward centers that are activated when we experience joy, love, or accomplishment are triggered. Dopamine levels rise rapidly. We feel genuinely good.[1]

Another study from 2023 found that firms that make mentorship a priority report higher employee satisfaction, stronger commitment, and greater innovation. But to be honest, you don't need data to confirm what your heart already knows: People do well when they feel noticed, supported, and believed in.[2]

In other words, giving back is more than just an outward gesture. It becomes an internal healing. It improves your mood, changes your perspective, and gives you a sense of purpose that no external achievement can replicate.

I've felt it firsthand. On days when the pressure felt overwhelming or the numbers didn't land exactly where we wanted them to, what grounded me wasn't the next big deal—it was the *people*. It was seeing someone I mentored land their first leadership position. It was watching a workshop attendee realize that financial freedom was within reach for them too.

Success built on service feels different. It *lasts*.

RIPPLE EFFECT OF EMPOWERMENT

For one of our early educational workshops, we had opened the doors to the public to provide a free training on the fundamentals of real estate investing—something that had felt so locked away and mysterious to me when I first started out as a businesswoman. Our goal was straightforward: to make financial literacy accessible, inviting, and human to everyone.

At the end of the training session, as people were mingling and packing their belongings, a woman approached me. She appeared nervous at first, gripping her notebook tightly to her chest.

When she finally spoke, her voice cracked with emotion.

She said, "This is the first time I've ever felt like this world could be for me."

I could feel the lump rise in my throat as her words sank in.

It wasn't about the numbers or the techniques we had taught; it was about belonging. It was about establishing a space where she felt seen, heard, and welcomed into a world that once seemed so far out of reach. That moment broke open something inside me. It reminded me that giving back doesn't necessarily mean writing a big check or launching a huge initiative.

Sometimes, the most effective way to give is simply sharing what you know with others—passing on the torch of knowledge, access, and encouragement to someone who has been standing outside the door, wondering if she truly belongs. Similar to how one candle may illuminate a thousand others without losing its own flame, empowering one individual sets off a whole series of events. The goal of success shifts from ascending a hypothetical staircase to helping one another get to the top.

Giving to others not only transforms their lives but also transforms yours. You change the energy in your surroundings. You cause a chain reaction that extends beyond your own vision. When we freely give those things generously without holding back, we empower people. We change trajectories. Knowledge is powerful. Access is powerful. Encouragement is powerful. We spark possibilities that ripple out for years to come.

We at Simplending Financial have seen this magic time and time again. A woman who embraces her confidence doesn't keep it to herself; she carries it into her future, family, and community. She becomes a mentor to others. Whether at home or at work, she shows up in different ways. Her achievements sow seeds of opportunity wherever she goes. And that's the lovely thing about empowerment: It spreads easily.

And watching other people get up because you created room for them? There is no more satisfying kind of success than this one.

EMBRACING YOUR COMPANY'S GENEROSITY

We at Simplending Financial do not believe that awards and balance sheets are the sole means to measure success. We believe that the true success is measured by the influence we have on the communities we serve. We realized from the beginning that our mission had to extend beyond the confines of our office. Real change happens when businesses and communities grow together, and we wanted to be part of that growth story.

From the beginning, we knew that community partnerships would be key. Collaboration multiplies impact, so we sought out organizations and groups that shared our passion for empowerment, education, and inclusion.

One way we demonstrate this is by sponsoring events for young entrepreneurs, particularly women and minorities who do not necessarily have the same opportunities or exposure. We always attend—whether it's a new business pitch night, a financial education summit, or a leadership development program. Our support goes beyond simply writing a check; we show up, offer mentorship, and share our resources to help them thrive.

Aside from events, we are quite excited about freely and extensively sharing the knowledge we have acquired in business. As a result, we provide free ebooks, resource guides, webinars, and even a podcast series in which we discuss the realities of business, investment, leadership, and personal development. We believe that access should be free, because everyone deserves the tools to build a life of purpose and freedom, not just those who can afford it.

But here's something essential to us: When we give back, it's not with the mindset of rescuing or fixing anyone. It means we are willing to listen, learn, and assist with open hands and hearts. We are working together rather than trying to save everyone. Our mission is always to provide people with the tools they need to recognize their own abilities, believe in their own intelligence, and realize that the success they seek is already within their reach.

Giving back not only makes a one-time difference, but it also plants seeds that grow over time: seeds of hope, confidence, opportunity, and transformation. And one of the most rewarding aspects of this journey has been watching those seeds grow.

REDEFINING SUCCESS: IMPACT OVER REVENUE

When I first started Simplending Financial, like a lot of entrepreneurs, I thought success would be measured in numbers—revenue milestones, client counts, market share. And don't get me wrong, *those numbers matter*. They help keep the lights on and the mission moving forward.

But over time, something deeper revealed itself: The real scoreboard wasn't the spreadsheets; it was the stories.

It was the woman who, after years of financial struggle, emailed to say she finally bought her first home. It was the young man who, after attending one of our workshops, launched his own business and hired others from his neighborhood. It was the mother who shared that because of what she had learned through one of our free resources, she could now teach her children about building wealth instead of fearing money.

Those moments are the true profits. They're the moments that remind us why we started in the first place.

At Simplending Financial, we measure success not just by the deals we close, but by the *doors we open* for others. Not by the awards we win, but by the *confidence we help others build.* Not by the size of our company, but by the *size of the dreams we empower.* We believe the legacy we're building isn't going to be etched into stock charts or profit margins—it's going to live in the hearts of the people we've impacted. It's going to ripple through communities we may never even visit, through lives we've touched simply by showing up, sharing what we know, and standing beside those climbing their own ladders.

Success to us is about significance. It's about creating something that outlives us, something that doesn't just make headlines—it makes *history.* Because at the end of the day, when the last deal is signed and the last email is sent, the real question is simple:

Who did we lift? Who did we empower? What lives did we help transform?

That's the legacy worth building. And that's the success worth chasing.

PRACTICAL CALL TO ACTION: HOW YOU CAN GIVE BACK

Here's the beautiful thing about giving back: You don't have to wait until you have "made it." You don't need millions in the bank, a huge platform, or a grand stage. You already have everything you need to make a difference right where you are, right now.

Here are just a few simple ways you can start today:

- Mentor someone who's just a few steps behind you.

- Share a piece of advice you had to learn the hard way.

- Encourage a coworker who's quietly doubting herself.

- Buy coffee for the person behind you in line.

- Leave an uplifting note for a stranger.

Small actions create big ripples. You never know how one kind word, one moment of encouragement, or one piece of guidance could completely shift the trajectory of someone's life.

I want to challenge you—yes, you, reading this right now—to ask yourself: *How can I give back today?*

Not someday. Not when it's more convenient. Not when you feel more "ready." Today. It could be something as simple as checking in on a friend you know is struggling. Offering a listening ear to a colleague. Volunteering a skill to help a local nonprofit. Sharing a book, a tool, or a resource that inspired you.

And when you give from a place of authenticity and heart, it unlocks something extraordinary—not just in the lives you touch, but inside of you, too.

You are someone's answered prayer. You are someone's lifeline. You are someone's reminder that goodness still exists in this world. So go ahead and light that spark. Start the ripple. Be the reason someone believes in possibility again. Because giving back isn't just a nice thing to do; it's how we build a life—and a legacy—that truly matters.

GIVING BACK WHEN YOU FEEL EMPTY

Not long ago, a friend of mine—a teacher navigating burnout and grief after losing a parent—told me she felt disconnected from her work, her purpose, and herself. She couldn't find the strength to give like she used to. But then, one day, a student left a note on her desk that simply said, "Thank you for seeing me." It reminded her that giving back doesn't always require grand gestures. Sometimes, just showing up—quietly, imperfectly, honestly—is an act of generosity in itself.

Here's the honest reality: There will be seasons when you feel depleted. Times when life presses hard on every side—when your body is tired, your mind is stretched, and your heart feels too bruised to offer anything more. In those moments, the idea of "giving back" can feel like one more demand on already fragile reserves. We often hear the phrase, "You can't pour from an empty cup." And while it holds truth, it can sometimes become a reason we disconnect entirely—from people, from purpose, from the very things that can actually refuel us.

Giving back doesn't always mean grand gestures or heavy lifting. When you're empty, it's not about pushing harder—it's about shifting how you give.

In emptiness, give gently. Give quietly. Give with intention.

You don't have to host an event or lead a movement. Even in depletion, there are ways to give that don't cost your peace. Sometimes giving looks like

- Saying a prayer for someone even when you don't have words for yourself

- Sending a kind text, not because you're overflowing with energy, but because you remember what loneliness feels like

- Letting someone go ahead of you in a queue

- Listening to someone who just needs an ear

- Offering a smile when the world feels heavy

These aren't acts of burnout—they're acts of being. They remind you that even in weakness, you are still connected. Still capable of love. Still able to plant seeds that matter. These small offerings can carry weight we'll never fully grasp.

What's most important is that your giving comes from a place of alignment, not obligation. When you feel empty, ask yourself: *What can I offer without losing myself? What kind of giving would nourish me, too?*

That might mean giving through presence instead of performance. Listening instead of leading. Resting so you can give again later with strength and clarity.

And here's the beauty: Sometimes, when you give while empty—not out of guilt, but from a soul-level desire to stay connected—you begin to feel full again. Not because your circumstances change immediately but because giving awakens something inside you. Something human. Something whole.

You don't have to feel full to be generous. You only have to be willing to give what is real. Even if it's just a moment. Even if it's just your breath. That, too, is sacred.

WHEN YOU GIVE, YOU GROW

At the end of the day, giving back isn't just a piece of the success puzzle; it *is* the puzzle. It's the heartbeat behind every meaningful achievement. It's the thread that ties purpose to progress.

Throughout this chapter, we've explored how real impact comes from sharing your time, your knowledge, your encouragement, your resources. We've seen that mentorship isn't just a nice bonus; it's a lifeline for someone who's searching for hope. And we've uncovered the beautiful truth that abundance isn't about clinging tightly to what you have. It's about opening your hands and letting it flow.

Because here's the secret: The more you give, the more you grow. The more you lift others, the higher you rise. The more light you shine, the brighter your own path becomes.

Success isn't measured by how much you keep; it's measured by how much you share. It's found in the lives you touch, the dreams you help ignite, and the legacy you build through simple, consistent acts of generosity.

So if you take one thing away from this chapter, let it be this: You have more to give than you realize. And when you do—when you pour into others—you set off a chain reaction of possibility, hope, and transformation that reaches far beyond anything you can imagine.

Start where you are. Give what you can. Watch what happens. Because the real magic of giving back? It doesn't just change the world around you; it changes you.

As we reflect on the power of giving back, it's clear that success is not just about what we achieve—it's about who we uplift along the way. But to give well, we must also live well. We must honor our limits, refill when we're empty, and align with the deeper current that gives our generosity meaning.

So, as we turn the page, let's dive into the idea of living in flow—the art of working, creating, and receiving with ease and purpose, where everything aligns and every action feels like it's part of a bigger, more meaningful journey.

REVIEW QUESTIONS

1. According to the chapter, how does true success differ from traditional views of success?

2. What foundational promise did the author make when starting Simplending Financial?

3. Why is giving back considered a crucial part of the company's mission, not just an afterthought?

4. How does giving back create a ripple effect according to the author?

5. What is the relationship between giving back and personal or business growth as described in the chapter?

6. What question does the author suggest we ask ourselves when evaluating our success?

7. List at least three practical ways you can give back today, as suggested in the chapter.

8. How can small actions create big ripples in other people's lives?

9. Why does the author emphasize starting to give back now rather than waiting until you "make it"?

10. In your own words, what does "building a legacy" mean based on the message of this chapter?

CHAPTER 17

LIVING IN FLOW

Have you ever been so immersed in something that time didn't matter? When everything felt easy and inspired? That's flow.

Living in flow is one of the most beautiful ways we can experience the fullness of receiving. It's not about hustling harder, pushing past every barrier, or tightly controlling outcomes; it's about stepping into a space where we trust that life, in its perfect timing, is always working for us.

Flow happens when you release the need to control every variable, every outcome, and every opportunity. It's when you shift from forcing results to creating the conditions for opportunities, resources, and the right people to find you. Instead of operating from resistance or rigid expectations, you stay agile, clear-minded, and open—ready to move with momentum when it appears.

And perhaps most powerfully, flow opens the channel to receive creativity. When you're no longer striving or overthinking, ideas arrive with greater ease. Inspired solutions, innovative concepts, and fresh perspectives begin to emerge—not from pressure but from presence. In flow, you don't chase creativity; you receive it.

In the financial lending world, we're trained to be strategic, persistent, and results-driven, and those qualities are absolutely essential.

But what often gets overlooked is the power of allowing space for innovation, collaboration, and unexpected growth. When you live and work in flow, you don't miss opportunities because you're too busy trying to control every detail. You're able to recognize them, seize them, and expand them.

Living in flow is one of the most effective ways to unlock sustainable success. It's not about being passive; it's about being intelligently responsive. It's about trusting the process you've built, adapting to real-time shifts, and remaining open to new avenues for growth that rigid planning could never predict.

Flow is where preparation meets adaptability. It's where strategy meets opportunity. It's where all the hard work you've invested starts to create real leverage—not because you forced the outcome but because you created the right environment for success to scale naturally.

In this chapter, we'll explore how embracing flow as a core leadership principle can dramatically increase not just what you achieve but what you're able to *receive*.

THE SCIENCE BEHIND LIVING IN FLOW

Living in flow is not just a concept grounded in philosophy or spiritual wisdom; it has scientific backing that shows how this state of being can positively impact both your mental and physical well-being. Flow, as first described by psychologist Mihály Csíkszentmihályi in the 1970s, refers to a mental state where a person is fully immersed in an activity with a sense of energized focus, full involvement, and enjoyment.[1] In this state, one is often working at their peak performance without feeling like they are forcing it.

The brain activity during flow is unique. Research has shown that during flow, there is an increase in dopamine, norepinephrine, and endorphins—neurotransmitters associated with positive emotions, motivation, and high levels of focus.[2] This combination of chemicals enhances creativity, boosts cognitive function, and improves problem-solving abilities. Interestingly, the part of the brain responsible for self-criticism and doubt—the prefrontal cortex—becomes less active, which allows for a more relaxed and confident state of mind. This means that when you are in flow, your brain is primed for optimal performance and reduced stress.

In terms of productivity and performance, research suggests that people in flow work faster, more efficiently, and with greater accuracy.[3] A study by the Flow Genome Project found that athletes, musicians, and entrepreneurs who experience flow consistently outperform their peers who do not experience it as frequently.[4] Flow states enable individuals to tap into their deepest reserves of creativity and skill, unlocking solutions that may not have been accessible during a more analytical, stressed state.

Understanding the science behind flow can help you leverage it to enhance your productivity and well-being as an entrepreneur. Embracing this state means acknowledging the science that supports your natural ability to thrive without force. So how can you start incorporating flow into your daily routine? What activities or practices help you get into your optimal state of focus and creativity? Try creating space for flow in your work and life, and observe how it transforms your approach to both business and personal challenges.

THE ART OF SURRENDER

Early on, I approached leadership with a tight grip. Every loan application, every team meeting, every marketing campaign was something I felt I had to personally oversee, down to the smallest detail. For example,

I once spent weeks micromanaging a new product rollout, including rewriting scripts, tweaking designs, and insisting on multiple layers of approval. Instead of empowering the team to innovate, the process dragged on, and we missed a prime market window. Another time, I was so focused on sticking to an original plan for a community partnership that I ignored emerging feedback from our clients. Had I listened sooner, we could have pivoted and created a service that was even better aligned with their real needs.

What I discovered was simple: Overcontrol doesn't lead to more success; it squeezes out opportunities that naturally want to emerge. Innovation thrives when leaders trust their structures, empower their people, and stay responsive to shifting market signals.

When we hear the word *surrender*, especially in financial industry, it can trigger a knee-jerk reaction. Surrender sounds like giving up. Like backing down. Like losing. But true surrender, when it comes to building a successful business and a fulfilling life, is actually a position of strength, not weakness. It's not about abandoning responsibility; it's about practicing strategic wisdom. It's about recognizing that growth and success aren't achieved through sheer force alone; they also come from learning when to step back, realign, and allow.

Surrender Means Releasing Rigid Plans

In business, it's smart to set goals, build systems, and plan for success. But it's just as smart to recognize when sticking too rigidly to a plan is actually limiting you. Markets shift. Client needs evolve. New technologies emerge. If we're too busy gripping yesterday's blueprint, we can miss the better opportunities standing right in front of us.

At Simplending Financial, some of our best growth moments have come from stepping away from rigid strategies and allowing space for fresh thinking. When we launched our new products, it wasn't because it was on a five-year plan; it was because we noticed client trends changing and allowed ourselves to adapt quickly rather than resist.

Surrender Means Releasing Ego

One of the hardest things to surrender is ego—the part of us that wants to be right, to be seen as competent, to have everything go exactly as we envisioned. Yet real growth rarely happens inside an echo chamber; it begins when we invite fresh perspectives to challenge us. True progress comes from the courage to admit we don't have all the answers—and from staying open to the possibility that the best ideas may come from the most unexpected places.

Some of the most valuable partnerships I've experienced came from situations I didn't engineer or control. They came from being open, from listening without a fixed agenda, and from allowing trust and mutual value to guide the relationship, not rigid negotiation tactics.

Surrender Means Releasing Hyper-Control

There's a fine line between leadership and micromanagement. True leadership requires trust—trusting the team you've built, the systems you've designed, and your own ability to adjust course as needed. Hyper-controlling every project or every conversation drains your energy and kills your momentum. Worse, it prevents talented people from stepping into their full potential.

One of the most powerful shifts we made inside Simplending was empowering our teams to own projects without needing every decision funneled back to leadership for approval. The more we trusted them, the more innovative and invested they became.

So, what does surrender have to do with flow? Flow, at its core, arrives when we stop trying to force every solution and start working with the energy of our business, not against it. It's the ability to recognize when the best strategy isn't pushing harder but adjusting faster. It's having the confidence to know that sometimes, stepping back is the most powerful move you can make.

Here are some signs that your business is working in flow:

Trusting the right clients will come: In the early stages of Simplending Financial, we said yes to every potential client, regardless of fit. If someone needed a loan, we adjusted our services, restructured our terms, and often bent over backward trying to meet impossible demands, believing that more clients meant more success.

That mindset is common, especially among female entrepreneurs, who often feel pressured to prove their value by being everything to everyone. But it created chaos: delayed closings, constant stress, and dissatisfied customers who didn't value our expertise.

Once we shifted to trusting that the right clients would come—the ones aligned with our mission and service standards—everything changed. Instead of chasing every lead, we refined our messaging, clarified who we best served, and started vetting clients based on shared values. Surprisingly, business grew stronger. Our team was more energized, and our client success stories multiplied. Surrendering the need to "catch everyone" allowed us to build a thriving, more sustainable firm.

Allowing unexpected partnerships to unfold: We had long relied on traditional networking and cold outreach to form partnerships, meticulously tracking every lead on spreadsheets and setting aggressive quarterly targets. But some of our most impactful partnerships didn't come from planned strategy at all.

For example, at a local women's leadership luncheon, a casual conversation with a fellow entrepreneur unexpectedly blossomed into a referral relationship that brought in high-quality clients for years. We hadn't forecasted it, budgeted for it, or mapped it on any business plan. It happened because we stayed open to genuine connection. That openness created space for the unexpected to reach us rather than us trying to force or chase it.

This is the power of receiving: When you create room in your business for things to come to you, you make space for aligned opportunities that structured planning can't always predict. Had we only focused on preapproved partnership models, we would have missed out on opportunities that were natural, powerful, and enduring.

Receiving solutions without engineering every detail: There was a time when I insisted on reviewing and controlling every step of every project, from marketing designs to client onboarding scripts. It exhausted the team and stifled creativity. Eventually, I realized that my need to control everything was actually blocking the brilliance around me. When I surrendered that grip and trusted the team to lead with their own expertise, better outcomes started to emerge.

One example was when a junior team member suggested streamlining our loan application process with a digital portal. I hadn't considered it because I was still focused on optimizing our older system. Her idea not only improved efficiency by 40 percent but also dramatically boosted client satisfaction scores.

That solution didn't come because I controlled every detail; it came because I surrendered my need to manage everything and allowed space for someone else's insight to rise. That's the power of surrender. It creates room for innovation, collaboration, and results that exceed what we could have scripted on our own.

Take a moment to reflect. Where in your business or life are you gripping too tightly? What one thing could you relax on or trust more today? Sometimes the smartest move isn't doing more; it's *allowing more.*

It's trusting that you've laid the right foundations and that when you make room, the right opportunities will step in.

RECEIVING SUPPORT AND COLLABORATION IN FLOW

Flow isn't just a personal state; it's a relational dynamic.

One of the biggest myths about entrepreneurship is that success is a solo journey, that it's all about the lone leader with a relentless work ethic. But in reality, true flow *invites* collaboration. When you're in flow, you're no longer clinging to control or operating from scarcity. You're open, and that openness creates fertile ground for others to step in, contribute, and multiply the impact.

I experienced this firsthand in the early days of Simplending Financial. I had the vision, the drive, and the plan, but it wasn't until I surrendered the need to carry it all alone and started collaborating with the right people that the company truly evolved. Sometimes it was a partner suggesting a more efficient process that saved us months of work; other times, it was a team member's insight that opened doors to a new client demographic we hadn't even considered.

When you stop forcing outcomes and start allowing solutions to emerge, you create space for unexpected collaboration. You begin to recognize that growth isn't just about what you can build with your own two hands; it's about what can unfold when you trust others to bring their expertise, energy, and creativity into the mix.

Sometimes support looks like a formal partnership or mentorship; other times, it's as simple as having someone to brainstorm with, someone who sees your blind spots, or someone who challenges your assumptions in the best way possible. By embracing collaboration, you shift from scarcity thinking—*If I don't do it myself, it won't be done right*—to a mindset of abundance—*Imagine what's possible when I don't have to do it all alone.*

Flow-enabled collaboration isn't about handing off tasks; it's about cocreating outcomes. It's about trusting that when you allow support in, you're not losing control—you're expanding possibility.

LIST THREE AREAS WHERE YOU COULD INVITE OR ACCEPT MORE SUPPORT THIS MONTH.

- What project could benefit from a second opinion?
- Where could you ask for administrative help or outsource a task?
- Who in your network might have insights you haven't tapped into yet?

RECEIVING OPPORTUNITIES

One of the most powerful shifts you can make as a businesswoman is recognizing that you don't have to say yes to every offer, every deal, or every partnership that crosses your path. Saying yes out of fear—fear of missing out, fear of disappointing others, fear of scarcity—can trap you in obligations that drain your energy and pull you off course.

Living in flow means receiving opportunities but with discernment, not desperation. Opportunities don't always knock when we're trying to force them. Often, they emerge when we are working steadily, staying open, and trusting the momentum we've built.

Discernment Is a Business Superpower

At Simplending Financial, I've learned to evaluate every opportunity with a simple filter:

- Does it align with our long-term vision?

- Does it bring real value to our clients or team?

- Does it feel expansive, not contractive?

When you're in flow, the answers to these questions surface more intuitively. You don't have to overanalyze or second-guess. And if the answer isn't a clear yes, it's often a strategic no.

Some of our best business decisions have come not from chasing the flashiest option but from listening inward and holding out for what felt truly aligned. Sometimes it's a quiet collaboration that leads to a breakthrough months later; other times, it's declining a tempting opportunity because it doesn't reflect our core principles and watching a better one arrive shortly after.

When you're in flow, you're no longer making decisions from fear, urgency, or ego. You're tuned in to yourself, your values, your mission, and from that alignment, your inner compass becomes sharper. You begin to sense what's truly aligned and what's just noise. This is the essence of discernment.

Receiving in flow means trusting that the right opportunities will continue to show up and that you have the wisdom to choose wisely.

FINDING CREATIVITY AND INNOVATION IN FLOW

In the fast-paced world of financial services, we often prioritize strategy, execution, and measurable results, and rightly so. But the truth is, creativity is just as critical to sustainable success. Whether you're designing new products, solving client challenges, or expanding into new markets, your ability to innovate determines your ability to lead.

The catch? Creativity can't be forced. It's not something you can schedule into a fifteen-minute slot between back-to-back meetings. True creativity is received. It arrives when your mind is open, energized, and willing to explore beyond the obvious. It's in moments of openness—not overanalysis—that new visions for your business emerge. When you're constantly pushing, creativity retreats. When you create space, creativity flows in.

Creativity flourishes in flow because you're fully present, deeply engaged, and internally aligned, which allows unexpected ideas and solutions to emerge with ease. Time fades, self-consciousness disappears, and the brain operates at its most creative and integrative capacity. Living in flow expands your ability to connect dots you hadn't seen before.

In my own journey, I've found that the best ideas come from creating space, surrendering control, and trusting that inspiration will arrive when I'm open to it. Whether it's a new marketing approach or a fresh vision for how we serve our clients, the most powerful insights have come when I allowed flow to lead the way. At Simplending Financial, some of our most successful service models weren't born out of strategy sessions or performance metrics; they emerged during moments of reflection: coffee chats without agendas, quiet weekends, and spontaneous conversations where creativity had room to breathe.

While moments of quiet or stillness aren't the flow state itself, they can lay the essential groundwork. Structured brainstorming has its place, but often, the best ideas surface during "unstructured" time. The key isn't to abandon structure altogether; it's to balance execution with openness, so you're not just operating the business you have but actively envisioning the one you could create next.

Schedule a weekly block with no agenda—just a notebook and an open mind. You'll be surprised what surfaces when you're not trying to produce on demand.

HOW FLOW LEADS TO ABUNDANCE

Remember from Chapter 15 that when we receive with gratitude, we can work from a place of overflow. One of the most powerful truths about living in flow is this: You rarely receive just enough. You often receive more than you expected.

Trying to tightly control every aspect of your growth often limits what's possible. Flow, on the other hand, creates conditions for expansion beyond your plans. When you stay open, act strategically, and remain available for new possibilities, you position yourself not just for success but for surplus.

When you stop forcing outcomes and start aligning with flow, opportunities, ideas, and connections multiply. You might set a clear goal, only to find that the results surpass what you initially envisioned. This is the phenomenon of overflow, where the outcomes are greater than the inputs. Overflow can take many forms:

- New client referrals you didn't even ask for
- Partnership opportunities landing in your inbox
- Innovative ideas appearing just when you need them
- Resources flowing to a project you were about to pause

At Simplending Financial, some of our biggest growth leaps weren't the direct result of five-year plans or exhaustive forecasts. They were the outcome of doing good work, staying visible, and remaining agile enough to say yes when unexpected opportunities came knocking.

Overflow doesn't mean sitting back passively; it means doing your part with excellence and then allowing room for things to evolve even better than expected. It's strategic alignment plus openness, not just hard-driving effort.

FLOW AS THE HIGHEST FORM OF RECEIVING

Think of life and business as a river—you are not here to fight against the current. Trying to control every twist and turn or paddling against the flow can lead to exhaustion and frustration. The key is to flow with the current: to trust that the path will unfold, often in ways you least expect.

As an entrepreneur, you've already demonstrated immense strength, resilience, and vision. But the next phase of growth isn't about working harder or pushing further; it's about aligning yourself with the flow of opportunity, allowing the river of your efforts to naturally carry you toward your destination.

Living in flow is the highest form of receiving. It is a state of ease, where opportunities, ideas, and support naturally align with your efforts. When you embrace flow, you stop seeing yourself as someone who must constantly chase success. Instead, you recognize that success is already in motion, and your role is to trust the process and position yourself to receive.

You don't have to force. You don't have to chase. Trust that you are already positioned to receive the next big step, the right partnership, or the breakthrough you've been working toward. All that's required now is to release the need for constant control and instead lean into the abundance that is already flowing toward you.

You are aligned with success. By embracing flow, you open yourself to receiving what's next—without the struggle.

As you move forward, remember: Life doesn't have to be a battle. Trust the current, trust the process, and trust yourself. You've got this.

I'll end this chapter with a challenge for you: Pick one day over the next month and label it your "Flow Day." No rigid to-do list. No packed back-to-back meetings. Instead, allow yourself to follow your energy and intuition. Spend time on activities that inspire you—whether that's brainstorming, deep conversations, creative work, or simply stepping away from your usual environment.

Notice what happens when you remove the pressure to produce. Notice how many ideas surface when your mind has breathing room. Flow isn't something you chase; it's something you allow. And sometimes, the most powerful thing you can do for your business is simply get out of your own way.

REVIEW QUESTIONS

1. How does the concept of "abundance" shift your approach to receiving support or opportunities in business?

2. What is the role of creativity in flow, and why is it important for sustainable success in business?

3. How does the myth of entrepreneurship as a solo journey contrast with the concept of collaboration in flow?

4. Reflect on a recent project or task—where could collaboration have led to more efficient or creative results?

5. What are the three key questions you should ask when evaluating an opportunity in flow?

6. Describe a time when saying no to an opportunity led to a better outcome. How did this demonstrate the power of discernment?

7. How can "unstructured" time, such as taking a break or engaging in informal conversations, lead to innovation and new ideas?

8. Why is it important to balance structured execution with openness in order to foster creativity and growth?

9. In what ways does living in flow lead to abundance, and how can this overflow positively impact your business?

10. Why is it important to balance structured execution with openness in order to foster creativity and growth? How can you align yourself with the flow of opportunities in your business, and what steps can you take to embrace this mindset in your day-to-day operations?

CHAPTER 18

FULL CIRCLE

You've made it to the end—but really, this is only the beginning. This journey—*She Believes, She Receives*—was never about checking off steps in a linear process. It's about embodying a new way of being. It's about learning to lead with intention, to show up with authenticity, and to trust your inner voice even when the world tells you otherwise.

When I first dreamed of Simplending Financial, it was just that—a dream. But what brought it to life was *clarity of thought, certainty of belief, courageous action*, and finally, *the willingness to receive*. That last part? It was the hardest for me. But I've learned that receiving isn't passive—it's an act of self-worth. It's saying, *I am open. I am ready. I am enough.*

This book is a love letter to every woman who has ever doubted her potential, dimmed her light, or played small to fit in. It's a reminder that you don't have to ask for permission to create the life you know you're meant to lead. You already have everything you need. The clarity. The belief. The drive. And now, the space to receive.

Think boldly. Believe fiercely. Act with purpose. And receive with grace.

You are the writer of your story and the architect of your life. You don't have to hustle your way to worthiness. You already *are* worthy. You don't have to chase abundance; you simply have to *allow it in*.

I'll leave you with this: What if everything you've ever wanted is already on its way to you—right now—and all that's left is for you to make room for it?

Make room.

Receive it.

And don't forget to pass it on.

With all my heart,

—JANINE CASCIO

NOTES

CHAPTER 1

1. Fiona Jerry, "The Science Behind Finding the Passion: Insights from Neuroscience," *Higher Education Review*, September 25, 2023, https://www.thehighereducationreview.com/design/news/the-science-behind-finding-the-passion-insights-from-neuroscience-nid-4387.html.

2. Jerry, "The Science Behind Finding the Passion."

3. Robert Vallerand, *The Psychology of Passion: A Dualistic Model* (Oxford University Press, 2015).

4. Vallerand, *The Psychology of Passion.*

5. Jessica Morales, "Two Types of Passion: Harmonious vs. Obsessive," *Psychology Today*, August 8, 2020, https://www.psychologytoday.com/us/blog/building-the-habit-hero/202008/two-types-passion-harmonious-vs-obsessive.

6. Julie Masters, "Gay Hendricks—The Big Leap—Finding Your Zone of Genius," *Inside Influence* (podcast), November 15, 2022, https://juliemasters.com/gay-hendricks-the-big-leap-finding-your-zone-of-genius/.

CHAPTER 2

1. Ian Boreham and Nicola Schutte, "The Relationship Between Purpose in Life and Depression and Anxiety: A Meta-Analysis," *Journal of Clinical Psychology* 79, no. 12 (December 2023): 2736–67, https://onlinelibrary.wiley.com/doi/full/10.1002/jclp.23576.

2. Flavia Chereches, Gudrun Godmundsdottir, and Gabriel Olaru, "Linking Sense of Purpose and Multiple Markers of Health in Older Adulthood: A Bidirectional Approach," *European Journal of Personality* (April 18, 2025), https://journals.sagepub.com/doi/10.1177/08902070251329072.

3. Majid Fotuhi, "The Science Behind the Powerful Benefits of Having a Purpose," *Practical Neurology* (September 2015), https://practicalneurology .com/diseases-diagnoses/alzheimer-disease-dementias/the-science-behind -the-powerful-benefits-of-having-a-purpose/30530/.

CHAPTER 3

1. Carol Dweck, Gregory Walton, and Geoffrey Cohen, "Academic Tenacity: Mindsets and Skills that Promote Long-Term Learning," Bill & Melinda Gates Foundation, 2014, https://ed.stanford.edu/sites/default/files/manual/ dweck-walton-cohen-2014.pdf.

2. Dweck, Walton, and Cohen, "Academic Tenacity."

3. Alyssa Reeder, "Anastasia Soare, Founder, Anastasia Beverly Hills," *Into the Gloss*, June 2015, https://intothegloss.com/2015/06/anastasia-soare -founder-anastasia-beverly-hills.

4. "Case Study: Ethique," Pledge Me, https://static1.squarespace.com/static/ 54b71357e4b0a3e130d374d8/t/5ec5c3370bf3c113a905a200/1590018897411/ Ethique_Case_Study_PledgeMe_Equity_Crowdfunding.pdf.

5. Catherine Cote, "Growth Mindset vs. Fixed Mindset: What's the Difference?" *Harvard Business School Online*, March 10, 2022, https://online.hbs.edu/blog/ post/growth-mindset-vs-fixed-mindset.

6. Ben Janse, "Ricardo Semler Biography, Quotes and Book," toolshero, September 17, 2024, https://www.toolshero.com/toolsheroes/ricardo-semler/.

7. Howard Schultz, *Onward: How Starbucks Fought for Its Life without Losing Its Soul* (Rodale Books, 2011).

8. Viktor Frankl, *Man's Search for Meaning* (Beacon Press, 2006).

9. Carol Dweck, *Mindset: The New Psychology of Success* (Random House, 2006).

10. Mark Moran, "Workplace Meditation: Boosting Corporate Productivity and Well-Being," American Institute of Health Care Professionals, July 12, 2024, https://aihcp.net/2024/07/12/workplace-meditation-boosting-corporate -productivity-and-well-being/.

11. Lara Hilton, Nell Marshall, and Susanne Hempel, "Mindfulness Meditation for Workplace Wellness: An Evidence Map," *WORK* 63, no. 2 (May 28, 2019), https://doi.org/10.3233/WOR-192.

CHAPTER 4

1. "Intentions Versus Goals," *Intelligent Change,* January 15, 2024, https://www
    .intelligentchange.com/blogs/read/intentions-vs-goals.

2. Joseph Arguinchona and Prasanna Tadi, *Neuroanatomy, Reticular Activating
    System* (StatPearls Publishing, 2025).

3. Peter Gollwitzer, "Implementation Intentions: Strong Effects of Simple Plans,"
    American Psychologist 54, no. 7 (July 1999): 493–503, https://www.researchgate
    .net/publication/232586066_Implementation_Intentions_Strong_Effects_of
    _Simple_Plans.

4. Vishen Lakhiani, "Arianna Huffington on the Pillars of Wellbeing," April
    28, 2018, in *Mindvalley Podcast* (podcast), https://podcast.mindvalley.com/
    transcript-12/.

5. Guy Raz, "Spanx: Sara Blakely," September 11, 2016, in *How I Built This with
    Guy Raz* (podcast), https://podcasts.apple.com/us/podcast/spanx-sara-blakely/
    id1150510297?i=1000396023160.

6. "Transcript of Oprah Winfrey: Intention," *Oprah's SuperSoul Conversations,*
    Podcasts by Happy Scribe, https://podcasts.happyscribe.com/oprah-s
    -supersoul-conversations/oprah-winfrey-intention.

CHAPTER 5

1. Srini Pillay, "Can Visualizing Your Body Doing Something Help You Learn
    to Do It Better?" *Scientific American,* May 1, 2025, https://www.scientific
    american.com/article/can-visualizing-your-body-doing-something-help-you
    -learn-to-do-it-better/.

2. Lisa Marshall, "Your Brain on Imagination: It's a Lot Like the Real Thing,
    Study Shows," *CU Boulder Today,* December 6, 2018, https://www.colorado.
    edu/today/node/31511.

3. Svetla Velikova and Bente Nordtug, "Self-Guided Positive Imagery Training:
    Effects Beyond the Emotions—A Loreta Study," *Frontiers in Human
    Neuroscience* 11 (January 2018), https://pubmed.ncbi.nlm.nih.gov/29375344/.

4. Velikova and Nordtug, "Self-Guided Positive."

CHAPTER 6

1. "Goal Setting: Turning Dreams into Achievable Plans," Advancing The Seed, Inc., July 29, 2024, https://www.advancetheseed.org/blog/goal-setting-turning-dreams-into-achievable-plans.

2. Elliott Berkman, "The Neuroscience of Goals and Behavior Change," *Consulting Psychology Journal* 70, no. 1 (March 2018), https://pmc.ncbi.nlm.nih.gov/articles/PMC5854216/.

3. Sarah Milne, Sheina Orbell, and Paschal Sheeran, "Combining Motivational and Volitional Interventions to Promote Exercise Participation: Protection Motivation Theory and Implementation Intentions," *British Journal of Health Psychology* 7, no. 2 (May 2002): 163–84, https://pubmed.ncbi.nlm.nih.gov/14596707/.

4. "Canva Announces USD 40 Billion Valuation Fueled by the Global Demand for Visual Communication," Canva, September 14, 2021, https://www.canva.com/newsroom/news/canva-announces-usd-40-billion-valuation-fueled-global-demand-visual-communication.

5. Laura Entis, "From an Extra Bedroom to 20 Stores and Counting: How Kendra Scott Created a Multimillion-Dollar Jewelry Empire," *Entrepreneur*, April 13, 2015, https://www.entrepreneur.com/growing-a-business/from-an-extra-bedroom-to-20-stores-and-counting-how-kendra/244921.

CHAPTER 7

1. Rebecca Aydin, "How 3 Guys Turned Renting Air Mattresses in Their Apartment into a $31 Billion Company, Airbnb," *Business Insider*, September 20, 2019, https://www.businessinsider.com/how-airbnb-was-founded-a-visual-history-2016-2.

CHAPTER 8

1. Andrew Fox et al., "Extending the Amygdala in Theories of Threat Processing," *Trends in Neurosciences* 38, no. 5 (April 4, 2015): 319–29, https://pmc.ncbi.nlm.nih.gov/articles/PMC4417372/.

2. Michael Merzenich, Thomas Van Vleet, and Mor Nahum, "Brain Plasticity-Based Therapeutics," *Frontiers in Human Neuroscience* 8 (June 2014), https://doi.org/10.3389/fnhum.2014.00385.

NOTES

3. Joseph LeDoux, "Rethinking the Emotional Brain," *Neuron* 73, no. 5 (March 8, 2012): 653–76, https://pmc.ncbi.nlm.nih.gov/articles/PMC3625946/.

4. Pauline Rose Clance, "The Imposter Phenomenon in High Achieving Women: Dynamics and Therapeutic Intervention," *Psychotherapy: Theory, Research & Practice* 15, no. 3 (1978), https://www.paulineroseclance.com/pdf/ip_high _achieving_women.pdf.

CHAPTER 10

1. Jeffrey McKinney, "With $1500 in Cash Janice Bryant Howroyd Became First Black Woman to Own a Billion-Dollar Company," *Black Enterprise*, February 1, 2023, https://www.blackenterprise.com/with-1500-in-cash-janice-bryant -howroyd-became-first-black-woman-to-own-a-billion-dollar-company/.

1. "Mary Barra," Forbes Profile, *Forbes*, https://www.forbes.com/profile/ mary-barra/.

CHAPTER 11

1. Mathieu Servant et al., "Neural Bases of Automaticity," *Journal of Experimental Psychology: Learning, Memory, and Cognition* 44, no. 3 (September 2017), https://pmc.ncbi.nlm.nih.gov/articles/PMC5862722/.

2. "Walt Disney," *Biography,* updated January 7, 2022, https://www.biography .com/business-leaders/walt-disney.

3. Emily Weiss, "'Like All Good Things, It Wasn't Always a Smooth Path': Emily Weiss Recounts the Highs & Lows of Building the Glossier Empire," *British Vogue*, November 2024, https://www.vogue.co.uk/article/ emily-weiss-glossier-interview.

4. Maya Angelou, "The Art of Fiction," interview by George Plimpton, *The Paris Review*, no. 116 (Fall 1990), https://www.theparisreview.org/interviews/2279/ the-art-of-fiction-no-119-maya-angelou.

5. Stephanie Strom, "At Chobani, Now It's Not Just the Yogurt That's Rich," *The New York Times*, April 26, 2016, https://www.nytimes.com/2016/04/27/ business/a-windfall-for-chobani-employees-stakes-in-the-company.html.

6. Ingrid Lunden, "How Atlanta's Calendly Turned a Scheduling Nightmare into a $3B Startup," *TechCrunch*, January 26, 2021, https://techcrunch

.com/2021/01/26/how-atlantas-calendly-turned-a-scheduling-nightmare-into-a-3b-startup/.

7. Ashley Lutz, "How Tory Burch Built a $3.5 Billion Company in Less Than a Decade," *Business Insider*, September 2014, https://www.businessinsider.com/tory-burch-success-story-2014-9.

CHAPTER 12

1. Stephanie Melhorn and Lindsay Cates, "Map: New Business Applications Surge Across the Country," *U.S. Chamber of Commerce*, February 2, 2024, https://www.uschamber.com/small-business/new-business-applications-a-state-by-state-view.

2. Chase Jarvis, "Payal Kadakia: Take the Leap, Start a Business," February 16, 2022, in *The Chase Jarvis LIVE Show* (podcast), https://chasejarvis.com/blog/take-the-leap-start-a-business-with-payal-kadakia/.

3. Ben Casnocha, "Reid Hoffman's Two Rules for Strategy Decisions," *Harvard Business Review*, March 5, 2015, https://hbr.org/2015/03/reid-hoffmans-two-rules-for-strategy-decisions.

4. Madeline Buxton, "Stitch Fix CEO Katrina Lake Talks About Leading a Public Company & Her Upcoming Maternity Leave," *Refinery29*, June 18, 2018, https://www.refinery29.com/en-us/2018/06/202050/katrina-lake-stitch-fix-amazon-maternity-leave.

5. Sissi Cao, "A Conversation with Sophia Amoruso, the 'Girlboss' Founder of Nasty Gal," *Observer*, October 2, 2018, https://observer.com/2018/10/sophia-amoruso-girlboss-nasty-gal/.

6. "Miki Agrawal of TUSHY On How To Get Past Your Perfectionism And 'Just Do It,'" *Authority Magazine*, November 7, 2021, https://medium.com/authority-magazine/miki-agrawal-of-tushy-on-how-to-get-past-your-perfectionism-and-just-do-it-30cd670add6d.

7. Emma Sandler, "Jessica Alba and CEO Nick Vlahos on The Honest Co.'s future: 'We will continue to innovate and pave the way,'" *Glossy*, May 10, 2021, https://www.glossy.co/beauty/jessica-alba-and-ceo-nick-vlahos-on-the-honest-co-s-future-we-will-continue-to-innovate-and-pave-the-way/.

8. Alison Rogish, Neda Shemluck, and Desiree D'Souza, "Leadership, Representation, and Gender Equity in Financial Services," *Deloitte Insights*, November 4, 2021, https://www.deloitte.com/us/en/insights/industry/financial-services/women-in-the-finance-industry.html.

CHAPTER 13

1. Randy Buckner, Daniel Schacter, and Jessica Andrews-Hanna, "The Brain's Default Network," *Annals of the New York Academy of Sciences* 1124, no. 1 (April 2008): 1–38, https://www.researchgate.net/publication/5451668_The_Brain's_Default_Network.

2. Hannah Owens, "This Is What Happens to Your Brain When You Do Therapy," *Verywell Mind*, May 25, 2024, https://www.verywellmind.com/how-therapy-can-change-your-brain-8650127.

3. Shian-Ling Keng, Moria Smosky, and Clive Robins, "Effects of Mindfulness on Psychological Health: A Review of Empirical Studies," *Clinical Psychology Review* 31, no. 6 (August 2011): 1041–56, https://pmc.ncbi.nlm.nih.gov/articles/PMC3679190/.

CHAPTER 14

1. Sarah Pressman, Tara Kraft, and Marie Cross, "It's Good to Do Good and Receive Good: The Impact of a 'Pay It Forward' Style Kindness Intervention on Giver and Receiver Well-Being," *The Journal of Positive Psychology* 10, no. 4 (July 2015): 293–302, https://www.researchgate.net/publication/276540202_It's_good_to_do_good_and_receive_good_The_impact_of_a_'pay_it_forward'_style_kindness_intervention_on_giver_and_receiver_well-being.

2. Adam Galinsky, "What Sets Inspirational Leaders Apart," *Harvard Business Review*, March–April 2025, https://hbr.org/2025/03/what-sets-inspirational-leaders-apart.

CHAPTER 15

1. Bradley Cannon, "All About Gratefulness with Robert A. Emmons, PhD," *Eye on Psi Chi* 21, no. 4 (Summer 2017), https://www.psichi.org/page/214EyeSum17cEmmons.

2. Michael Dill, "Win Wall—Celebrate Your Wins," Business Coach Michael Dill, https://www.businesscoachmichaeldill.com/win-wall-2/.

3. Effie Webb, "Stripe's CEO Has Customers Join Manager Meetings to Share Feedback—and Elon Musk Says It's a 'Good Idea,'" *Business Insider Africa*, April 11, 2025, https://africa.businessinsider.com/news/stripes-ceo-has-customers-join-manager-meetings-to-share-feedback-and-elon-musk-says/9pl8zxt#google_vignette.

CHAPTER 16

1. Elizabeth Svoboda, "Scientists Find That We Are Hard-Wired for Giving," University of Notre Dame College of Arts and Letters, September 5, 2013, https://generosityresearch.nd.edu/news/hard-wired-for-giving/.

2. Motsami John Modise, "The Impacts of Employee Workplace Empowerment, Effective Commitment and Performance: An Organizational Systematic Review," *International Journal of Innovative Science and Research Technology* 8, no. 7 (July 2023), https://www.researchgate.net/publication/376260679_The _Impacts_of_Employee_Workplace_Empowerment_Effective_Commitment _and_Performance_An_Organizational_Systematic_Review.

CHAPTER 17

1. Mihály Csíkszentmihályi, *Flow: The Psychology of Optimal Experience* (Harper & Row, 1990).

2. Dimitri van der Linden, Mattie Tops, and Arnold Bakker, "Go with the Flow: A Neuroscientific View on Being Fully Engaged," *European Journal of Neuroscience* 53, no. 4 (November 2020), https://pmc.ncbi.nlm.nih.gov/articles/ PMC7983950/.

3. Jussi Palomäki et al., "The Link Between Flow and Performance Is Moderated by Task Experience," *Computers in Human Behavior* 124 (June 2021), https:// www.researchgate.net/publication/352253579_The_link_between_flow_and _performance_is_moderated_by_task_experience.

4. Flow Genome Project, www.flowgenomeproject.com

ABOUT THE AUTHOR

JANINE CASCIO is the CEO and founder of Simplending Financial, a national private lending firm based in Houston that empowers real estate investors with innovative financing solutions. A visionary entrepreneur and conscious leader, Janine has built a company rooted in culture, collaboration, and bold execution—while championing women and underrepresented voices in the lending and real estate industries.

In addition to leading Simplending Financial, Janine is the founder of She Funds Academy, a fast-growing educational platform where women learn to fund, lead, and rise. Through her work, she is on a mission to redefine what success looks like in entrepreneurship: one built on self-discipline, mindset mastery, and purpose-driven leadership.

Janine is known for her refreshing blend of business acumen, authentic storytelling, and fearless innovation. Her writing invites readers to embrace possibility, trust their intuition, and create lives and companies rooted in both ambition and ease.